ADIY

ADIYOGI

ADIYOGI

THE SOURCE OF YOGA

SADHGURU
& ARUNDHATHI SUBRAMANIAM

HARPER
element

First published in India in 2017 by Harper Element
An imprint of HarperCollins *Publishers* India

Copyright © Sadhguru 2017

P-ISBN: 978-93-5264-392-9
E-ISBN: 978-93-5264-393-6

2 4 6 8 10 9 7 5 3

Sadhguru asserts the moral right
to be identified as the author of this work.

The views and opinions expressed in this book are the author's own and
the facts are as reported by him, and the publishers are not in
any way liable for the same.

The chapter 'Face-to-Face with the Axis of the World' was first published in
Himalaya: Adventures, Meditations, Life, edited by Ruskin Bond and
Namita Gokhale, Speaking Tiger Books, 2016.

HarperCollins *Publishers*
A-75, Sector 57, Noida, Uttar Pradesh 201301, India
1 London Bridge Street, London, SE1 9GF, United Kingdom
Hazelton Lanes, 55 Avenue Road, Suite 2900, Toronto, Ontario M5R 3L2
and 1995 Markham Road, Scarborough, Ontario M1B 5M8, Canada
25 Ryde Road, Pymble, Sydney, NSW 2073, Australia
195 Broadway, New York, NY 10007, USA

Typeset in 12/15.2 Adobe Jenson Pro
By Saanvi Graphics Noida

Printed and bound at
Thomson Press (India) Ltd

CONTENTS

PART TWO: CHRONICLES
SADHGURU

PART THREE: DIALOGUES
ARUNDHATHI SUBRAMANIAM

BEFORE THE BEGINNING

Arundhathi Subramaniam

'It's time to do a book on Adiyogi,' Sadhguru says one day.

I try to look interested.

'Adiyogi,' he repeats. 'Shiva.'

I nod.

'It doesn't interest you?' he says quizzically. It is more statement than question.

Since I have learnt over the years that it is difficult to conceal most things from this person who has become my guru, I launch into a tactful explanation. 'Of course, Shiva is the most enigmatic god in this subcontinent,' I begin.

'He isn't a god,' Sadhguru says crisply.

I know he enjoys playing contrary. I do too. But today I am determined to remain non-reactive. I opt for a poet's approach. 'It's true he's an inspired symbol for the dance of life and death. And as the cosmic dancer, he distils concepts of time, space, motion and velocity into stupendous iconography.' I grow more fluent as I warm up to my theme.

'He's much more than that,' Sadhguru cuts in. 'And his legacy isn't limited to this subcontinent.'

1

'Why not a book on you?' I say in a flash of inspiration. 'A book on a *living* yogi?' Having written Sadhguru's life story, I know there is still much of his unimaginably eventful inner life that remains undocumented.

'He's the world's first yogi. The only yogi. The rest of us are just his sidekicks.'

I decide I've spent enough time on diplomacy. I plunge into argument. 'There's just too much Shiva in the air. It's an epidemic. Calendar art, television serials, pop literature, science fiction. He's everywhere. Why keep harping on our ancient heritage? It's all too zeitgeisty. Too revivalist. Let's talk about something here and now. We don't need another book on Shiva.'

'He's here and now,' Sadhguru says quietly.

I pause.

'He's my fifty per cent partner in everything I do.'

I have heard Sadhguru say this before, but this time it seems less rhetorical. After twelve years around him, I am not entirely unused to the gnomic utterances of mystics. Sadhguru's deepest insights, I've discovered, are invariably tossed off mid-sentence, in parentheses, or as a throwaway line in a conversation. The remark is so casual now that I sense gravitas. I grow alert.

'Metaphorically, you mean?'

The question stays unanswered.

'He's here and now?' I repeat.

'He's my life breath.'

And that is, I suppose, when I give in.

It's not that I understand what I'm getting into. But I console myself with simple logic. While he can be infuriatingly unreasonable on occasion, Sadhguru still remains the most interesting person I know. Which means his fifty per cent partner can't exactly be tedious company.

And so, this is a book on Adiyogi.

But it is not as simple as that. Let me explain. This book is not an exercise in scholarship. Neither is it a work of fiction. Instead, this book is, for the most part, a kind of spiritual stenography. In short, a living guru becomes a channel or conduit for Shiva or Adiyogi.

A channel? The word can be disconcerting, I'm aware. Let us return to the word later.

For now, let me qualify that while it was not based on conventional research, the library was certainly an important source of material for this book. Except that it was a mystical library, not a material one.

On his annual sojourns to Mount Kailash in the Himalayas, Sadhguru seems to replenish his already considerable understanding of Adiyogi, his life and his work. And so, it is not a coincidence that many of the conversations that provided fodder for this book actually unfolded on a journey to this enigmatic mountain in Tibet.

Other reference points were the yogic tradition and the already sumptuous resource of Indian myth. But even here, it was Sadhguru who played the dual roles of medium and yogi. And for him, there was really no contradiction – one role was a seamless extension of the other. For yoga, he often says, is not for him an acquired knowledge system. It is the wisdom of his marrow, his bloodstream. An internalized wisdom. The mode by which he received it was not instruction. It was transmission – an ancient mode of spiritual pedagogy. That makes him a living archive – except that this is a man who is incapable of being turgid or pedantic. For me, he is always a reminder that mystical wisdom can be recognized by how lightly it is worn. He wears his with the careless panache with which he drapes his handwoven shawls.

'I am not spiritually educated,' he has often reiterated. 'I don't know any teachings, any scriptures. All I know is myself. I know this piece of life absolutely. I know it from its origin to its ultimate nature. Knowing this piece of life, one knows, by inference, every other piece of life. This is not sorcery; this is science – the science of yoga available to everyone who cares to look inward.'

And if Adiyogi is the primordial yogi, and even Sadhguru his sidekick, what does that make me? For the most part, I was just a stupefied scribe, vaguely aware that it was a privilege to be present as a unique mystical download took place.

I use the word 'unique' with care. Let me say at the start that I'm uncomfortable with tourist brochure idiom, the sticky superlatives of propaganda, whether commercial, political or religious. But there is no doubt in my mind that Sadhguru's utterances on Shiva add up to an unusual document. Strange, but unique.

But first, let's map the terrain.

Shiva – or Adiyogi, as Sadhguru prefers to call him (in accordance with the yogic tradition to which he is heir) – has been seen as the Ur-divinity of the world: wild, pagan, indefinable. He is apparently older than Apollo, the Olympian god of the Greeks, with whom he shares several characteristics as healer, archer, figure of beauty, harmony and light, symbolic of the sun, contemplation and introversion. He seems older too than Dionysus, the other Greek deity who shares many of his characteristics as the god of ecstatic delirium, dance, libido, intoxication, dissolution, protector of the freedoms of the unconventional, divine conduit between the living and the dead. Shiva has been seen as supreme godhead, folk hero, benevolent boon-bestower, shape-shifter, trickster, hunter, hermit, cosmic dancer, creator, destroyer. The epithets are endless.

There is no dearth of literature on Shiva. He has been the subject of passionate paeans by the saint poets of India down the centuries. He has been the subject of esoteric texts and metaphysical treatises all over the subcontinent. In recent times, he has been fictionalized, re-mythicized, sometimes bowdlerized, New-Agey-fied. But, oddly enough, he seems more in vogue than ever.

Far too elemental to be domesticated, he's more emblem than god, more primordial energy than man. Pan-Indian calendar art continues to paint him in the language of hectic devotion and lurid cliché: blue-throated, snake-festooned, clad in animal skin, a crescent moon on his head. Sometimes he is presented in a cosy picture as a beaming family man with wife and children, all of whom stand aureoled in a giant lemon of a halo. While this pop idiom is not without its own charm, everyone, including the average Indian, is aware that there is more to Shiva than that.

No one can quite define who or what he is. But we all instinctively know him as the feral, tempestuous presence that has blown through the annals of sacred myth since time out of mind. Philosophers, poets, mythologists, historians, novelists, Indologists, archaeologists have all contributed to the avalanche of Shiva literature down the centuries. It is a literary inheritance of considerable magnitude and no mean import.

Immense. Powerful. Turbulent. And more than a little terrifying. I confess that's how I've always seen him.

Sadhguru, however, is neither metaphysician nor mythologist. And that, I believe, is what makes this document distinct. Sadhguru's take on Shiva is a yogi's take on the progenitor of yoga. This is the portrait of the world's first guru by a living guru, a chronicle *of* the source of mysticism *by* a mystic.

That makes this a far more unpredictable enterprise than I had anticipated. To be present during the making of this book was somewhat bewildering. It is true that I oscillated between interlocutor and editor-archivist, snipping and suturing, tweaking and fine-tuning accounts from Sadhguru's many conversations and discourses. But for the large part, I was eavesdropper, my ear pressed to the narrative, as Sadhguru expounded a tale that was ancient and alive all at once.

But that was one half of the story.

The other half, I admit, was vexation. I wrestled with this material a great deal. I plied Sadhguru with questions, reminded him of loose ends and ragged edges, asked him to qualify, clarify, demystify. Sometimes that worked, sometimes it didn't. I accused him internally of being inconsistent. 'You speak of Shiva as a yogi and as formless energy, as symbol and no-thing,' I said. 'How on earth are we going to piece together a coherent story from so many fragments?'

It has been challenging trying to make my peace with Shiva – and I'm not done yet. But it has felt more challenging still to make my peace with the piecemeal.

Gradually, I began to align myself with the emerging architecture of this text. The form is prose, but the logic poetry. When a mystic tries to find a vocabulary to speak of the unfathomable, it is probably unfair to expect solar logic, pasteurized reason. Sadhguru often starts out with linearity and coherence, and suddenly resorts to a language that is cryptic and fragmentary. He begins with popular legend, swerves into fable, and suddenly spins out a yogic tale. His ability to make myth seem like current affairs – and vice versa – initially bothered me. Until I realized that this could well be the strength of his narrative. For like all mythic stories, this one is meant to be approached intuitively. The rationale is, as always, nocturnal (the realm of myth being the realm of 'public dream', as mythologist Joseph Campbell so memorably reminds us). It is a rationale we intuit even before we understand.

Sadhguru's own words helped put things in perspective. In a conversation, he once discussed the concepts of chaos and order as complementary rather than contrary. 'People assume that a jungle means disorder and a garden spells order,' he said. 'I use the word "jungle" to mean a very superior, highly sophisticated order. You don't see any straight lines, but still everything is in place. The order of the jungle is not logically correct. For a gardener, a jungle may look chaotic. But no, there is a very deep order in this chaos. A forest will live for millions of years, while a garden may not even last a month without maintenance.'

That gave me a clue as to how to approach this book. Rather than clip and prune Sadhguru's reflections into a tidy narrative, I realized the roughness of the frame was not just inevitable, it was actually appropriate. When it came to Adiyogi, it was absurd to expect a manicured prose garden. It had to be a teeming tropical jungle, a romp through cogency and chaos, folklore and arcana, myth and madness.

It was absurd, I realized, to expect a staid book from Sadhguru who is most emphatically not a staid yogi. Or from Adiyogi, who, by the looks of it, wasn't a staid yogi either. (In fact, 'staid yogi', I'm beginning to realize, is most definitely an oxymoron.)

When I stopped trying to look for bulletproof consistency, life became easier. This is not an immaculate text. Nor does it aspire to be. It is instead an exuberant kaleidoscope of glimpses. Glimpses of Adiyogi the way Sadhguru sees him – as pathfinder, outlaw, symbol, archetype, yogi, guru, living presence, ecstasy, emptiness.

Because its ambit is audacious, it is also doomed to failure. But perhaps failure isn't such a calamity, after all. My curiosity was first piqued when I heard Sadhguru describe himself as a failure. 'My dream is to enlighten the world, so I am bound to die a failure,' he said. 'But I will die a blissful failure. I can promise you that.'

That sounded like the kind of defeat to aspire to. And so the architecture of this book is jagged, the mosaic serrated, the jigsaw necessarily incomplete. It does not offer conclusions. It is not a biography of the world's first yogi. It is more an invocation. But since it is an invocation by a yogi, it is not just a panegyric, a poem of praise. I believe it carries a touch – as many Sadhguru-related endeavours do – of alchemy.

That alchemy, I have learnt over the years, is the distinguishing mark of any authentic spiritual guide. Without that, Sadhguru would be a yoga instructor. With it, he becomes a master.

In August 2011, I stood with others beside Sadhguru in front of Mount Kailash, the legendary abode of Shiva in the Tibetan Himalayas. It was then that I heard him speak again of the Jain mystic, Rishabha, who had come there centuries ago. 'He tried to download this immensity of wisdom that is Shiva. And, finally, he had to concede. He merged with this magnitude, this live mystical mountain. There is no other way.'

It was yet another reminder of the legacy of joyful failures to which we are heir. It suddenly felt all right to add one more unfinished tribute to the roaring cascade of Shiva chronicles that have drenched, revived and awed listeners since what seems like the dawn of time.

Things fell into place. If Sadhguru was the channel and medium for Shiva, I was content to play sidekick to the sidekick. My business was to ask my questions (spiritedly, if I chose – Adiyogi didn't seem to mind), and make room for words as well as silences. My job was to listen, to allow Sadhguru to speak. And Adiyogi to take over.

This is perhaps the right moment to address some fundamental questions, some invariable misgivings. The rest of the book explores who Adiyogi is: it clears misconceptions, adds new mysteries, unravels old ones. But who, one might ask, is the channel and revealer of Adiyogi in this book? What makes him a channel? And how are we meant to read this account? As fact or as fantasy? As verity, or as one more homegrown tale in a culture that spins out a myth a minute?

And, above all, who exactly *is* Sadhguru?

There are many ways to answer that question. One is the ritual litany: yogi, mystic, visionary, spiritual leader. The author of yoga programmes of antiquity and contemporary relevance. Public speaker. Environmentalist. Educationist. The founder of Isha, a spiritual organization with centres around the world. There are other avatars: golfer, trekker, poet, motorcyclist, scuba diver, aviator.

The chronicle I wrote of his life offers other perspectives. It tells the tale of the boy who grew up with mountains in his eyes, and only years later realized what those mountains meant. It traces the journey of a wild motorcyclist who turned mystic, an agnostic who turned spiritual master. What sustained me when documenting that incredible story was the fact that Sadhguru never asked for belief. I took my cue from his mock serious disclaimer at the very start: 'You'd be foolish to believe this story.' That was followed by the laughing caveat: 'You'd be even more foolish to disbelieve it.'

Born in Mysore in southern India, to a physician father (an ophthalmologist with the Indian railways) and devout mother, he grew up a wild and incorrigible prankster. A chronic truant at school, he recalls that much of his boyhood was spent roaming the forests, catching snakes, fishing, trekking, cycling, or simply sitting on trees and vacantly staring into space for hours on end. There was nothing remotely 'other-worldly' about him. On family visits to the temple, he preferred to remain outside. He often observed that those who came out of restaurants wore more contented expressions than those emerging from temples. 'In the Divine versus Dosa contest, the dosa is clearly the winner!' he often quips.

His obstinately individual streak persisted during his years as an undergraduate in English Literature at Mysore University. A certain spirit of empathy, however, led him to align himself with various politically revolutionary movements and causes. It was 'the era of blue jeans and the Beatles', as he often puts it, and he describes himself as 'a dry sceptic, a rock and roller, utterly uninfluenced by the religion or culture around me'. He devoured his Kafka, Dostoevsky and Camus with the same fierce passion with which he plunged into his motorcycle expeditions across the length and breadth of the country. When he found he needed money to fund his travels beyond the Indian border, he decided to try his hand at poultry farming, and later at a construction business. The profits rolled in: his petrol tank was full, the future seemed promising, and the present idyllic.

But at the age of twenty-five, something happened that not merely threw his plans into disarray, but consigned them to permanent oblivion. He rode up Mysore's Chamundi Hill one afternoon, a young man with time to kill, and returned several hours later, a yogi. When he speaks of that turning point in his life, he often says, 'I was sitting on a particular rock. I had my eyes open, not even closed. And something began to happen. Suddenly, I did not know which was me and which was not me. The air that I was breathing, the rock on which I was sitting, the atmosphere around me, everything had become me. The more I say it, the crazier it will sound, because what was happening was indescribable. What was me had become so enormous, it was everywhere. I thought this lasted a few minutes, but when I came back to my normal senses, it was about seven thirty in the evening. Over four hours had passed, my eyes were open, the sun had set, and it was dark. I was fully aware, but what I had considered to be myself until that moment had just disappeared. Tears were flowing to the point where my shirt was wet, and I was ecstatically crazy. When I applied my logical mind to it, the only thing it could tell me was that I was losing my balance. But it was so beautiful that I knew I didn't want to lose that experience.'

When he emerged, he knew that what had transpired, inexplicable as it was, was without doubt 'the most beautiful thing that can happen to a human being'. The sceptic had turned mystic.

And he knew life would never be the same again. 'I saw it was possible to be naturally ecstatic without any reason at all. My whole effort since then has been to somehow rub this experience off on other people.'

Lifetimes of memory descended in subsequent weeks. He now realized his experience was just a prologue to a far more important narrative. The condition of ecstatic freedom – the goal of every spiritual aspirant – was not unknown to him. It had already happened three lives ago. The crux of the narrative lay elsewhere. It lay in a promise made to a guru three lifetimes ago, a painful, unfulfilled promise. He had expended three lives trying to honour that pledge. That pledge gave this present lifetime a new impetus, a new sense of purpose. His only mission now, he realized, was to consecrate the Dhyanalinga.

What *was* the Dhyanalinga?

A subtle energy form, with seven primary chakras, or energy centres, operating at their optimal capacity, the Dhyanalinga was a feat that demanded considerable yogic prowess. Prowess, however, had not been in short supply. An adept of no mean calibre in his previous lives, schooled in the ancient tradition of kriya yoga, he had already attained considerable mastery over the human energy system.

The issue was social. Since the process entailed the participation of men and women in close proximity, the consecration of the Dhyanalinga had always been fraught with social opposition. Incomprehension and outright hostility had plagued all the previous attempts to create this energy form. This time, however, failure was not an option. Haunted by lifetimes of failure, he knew he had no time to lose. With a growing band of fiercely committed disciples, he began to address that unfinished aspiration yet again.

In 1999, after several eventful and turbulent years during which he almost lost his life, he emerged successful. The Dhyanalinga – an imperishable energy form, capable of sowing the seed of moksha, ultimate liberation, in all who sit in its precincts – was finally established at the foothills of the Velliangiri Mountains in southern India through *prana pratishtha*, an ancient yogic process of direct energy consecration.

Sadhguru has often described the Dhyanalinga as Shiva himself in his ultimate energy avatar. This is not Shiva as god or idol, but as a profound abstract representation – the *linga*, the primordial form. 'The Dhyanalinga was an invitation to bring down the highest entity of all,' says Sadhguru. 'He now stands there, available on every level to those who seek him.'

Viewed from this perspective, Sadhguru's entire life story is a reminder that his connection with Adiyogi is, in fact, a covenant of lifetimes – 'a crazy love affair', as he once put it.

Once, when I asked him about the source of his knowing about Adiyogi, his reply was crisp and matter-of-fact. Sadhguru is always quick to assert that mysticism is science, not wizardry. 'It is quite simple, really,' he said. 'Just as there is an internet, there is an "inner net". This is familiar to anyone who has looked deeply inward. The way the individual is made is the way the cosmos is made. Both come from the same manufacturing unit. It is in the lap of that same darkness or emptiness that everything is born. All the work that has ever been done in the realm of consciousness endures. And it can be accessed. This "inner net", or "introscope", is my guide. It empowered me to consecrate the Dhyanalinga. It has offered me access to various aspects of Adiyogi's wisdom and knowing when I have required it.'

On an earlier occasion, he had said, 'When my guru touched me on the forehead with his staff, what could not be learnt in lifetimes was transmitted in a moment. Since then, on the existential level, whatever I have needed to know has been available to me when I have needed it. On a daily basis, I do not carry the burden of this knowing. People usually become heavy and serious with knowledge.

But when knowing is transmitted as energy, not memory, the burden of knowledge is not on you.'

And so, being a 'channel' for Adiyogi is not an exalted self-appellation; it is for Sadhguru the result of lifetimes of dismantling the self, as we know it – of honing personal receptivity to the point where one can tune into what the poet Rilke once so evocatively called 'the news that is always arriving out of silence.' 'If you don't make yourself important within yourself,' Sadhguru often says, 'you can turn this body into a powerful instrument of perception and knowing. You could download the very language of creation, the deepest mysteries of the cosmos. There is nothing special about it. It is not some great achievement. All it takes is paying some attention to one's interiority. This is possible for everyone.'

Much has changed since the accomplishment of his life's mission. Sadhguru's life has been less ferociously single-pointed since then, although no less intense. As the founder of Isha, an international organization with human well-being as its core commitment, he has speaking engagements and programmes that take him around the world. It is a punishing schedule that he seems to negotiate with a yogi's unflappable élan. He is now an influential global spiritual leader.

But what is the 'guru' stuff about really?

It is perhaps best to confront the issue squarely. Let's start by acknowledging the reservations that the word provokes in so many of us. There's no denying that the word is suspect in most lexicons. For many, it is infected beyond redemption. For others, it's taken on a sinister, almost medieval ring. Tell people that you have a guru and watch the reactions. It's a word that makes acquaintances blink, relatives smile brightly, and friends enquire after your bank balance and love life in tones of deep solicitude. Many prefer to simply change the subject – hurriedly – as if to spare you the embarrassment of saying more.

I once happened to mention to an elderly colleague at a cultural centre I worked in that I wrote poetry. She smiled kindly. Before she left the room, she offered words of solace: 'I know you'll make something of your life one day.' I thanked her, wishing that I could say I'd invented toothpaste, turned down a job at NASA or even written a novel. But *poetry*?

I'm glad I've never had to tell her about having a guru.

But never mind colleagues. Let me admit to my own issues with spiritual commissars and paternalistic figures, with all attempts at straitjacketing the sacred. I often ask myself how on earth I landed up with a guru.

Perhaps the truest answer to that is I don't see myself as a sceptic who turned devotee. And if I consider Sadhguru to be my guide, it is because he has never asked me to give up one and embrace the other. The ratio varies. I am sometimes more doubter than disciple. Or, to put it more accurately, there are times when I'm more fearful than wondering, more distracted than committed, more resistant than receptive. At other times, I'm the reverse.

But the content of my doubts, fears and distractions has changed. And my questions have shifted. And beneath them is a bedrock of trust.

Which brings me to my second answer: I suspect I landed up with a guru because he is the only person I know who is more committed to my freedom than I am myself.

For many inspired by him, Sadhguru is a sage of unfathomable proportions. For those who don't quite see him that way, I believe this book can still be a chance to glimpse another perspective, dip into another world view, even if it isn't quite one's own.

I approach Sadhguru as my guru. But for all my self-avowed discipleship, I am as incapable of writing a hagiography as I am of writing an exposé. The world would often have us believe that we have no other option. But surely to limit ourselves to either-or is to consign ourselves to an eternal adolescence? Surely there are choices other than magisterial scorn or trite faith, revilement or rhapsody, castigation or canonization?

What often guided me in my writing of his life story – a tale that often left me incredulous – was Sadhguru's own unequivocal remark, 'Don't look up to anything, don't look down on anything.' It resonated deeply with me when I first heard it, given my own long-standing mistrust of hierarchy. It still comes to my rescue time and again.

The only response to mystery, I've realized, doesn't have to be suspicion or submission. Other options exist. Curiosity. A willing suspension of disbelief. Receptivity that doesn't lapse into gullibility. Enquiry that doesn't freeze into conclusion.

I enjoy listening. Not uncritically. And I am often happy to defer to disagreement as well. I like the mix of the rational and the non-rational that Sadhguru is capable of whipping up. In this account, it is true the latter predominates. At times, I receive it as a fascinating tale. At other times, I question. Much of the time, I don't entirely understand. But I prefer not to dismiss. Not just because there are 'more things on heaven and earth, Horatio…' (and *Hamlet* has often come to my aid in my interactions with Sadhguru), but because there is an essential kernel of trust.

That trust didn't blossom overnight.

Let me rewind. And this rewinding is strictly for readers who, like me, are seekers, who grapple with the reluctance to relinquish autonomy, and the fear of compromising their freedom.

'Why a guru? Why can't you learn from life?' a spirited young woman asked me after a reading in London. It was a question after my own heart. I might have asked it at one time.

I could have replied that a guru unlocks those parts of you that are shut, sealed, forgotten, and unavailable to life. He helps open doors that you were too scared to open, as well as doors you never knew existed. And those aren't the portals customarily uncovered by a psychotherapist.

But I knew that the urgency of her question merited a longer, fuller answer. In a tangential way, this book might be a response to that question.

When I met Sadhguru in 2004, I knew a few things about myself. I knew that I found most of my answers in poetry and the arts. I knew I was lucky to be earning a living doing largely what I enjoyed. The boundaries between work and play were happily blurred. Life in the big city of Bombay/ Mumbai/ Bambai, that city of many names and faces, was full, frantic, absorbing. I enjoyed its variousness, its vibrancy, its unexpectedness.

But there were also many things I didn't know about myself. I thought poetry would eventually fill in the blanks. But poetry was also *about* blanks. I hadn't quite bargained for those. It took me a long time to understand that poetry was a dark art because it was, in fact, a perforated utterance.

As a child, when I turned to poetry, it was with a sense of wonder at the giddy spin and bump of language in motion. The texture of language – now whipped cream, now gritty granola, suddenly Dacca muslin – spelt pure sensuous delight.

But then life intervened. And, gradually, the wonder diminished. Several friends from the cultural world seemed invested in the sameness too. We told ourselves we led the creative life. And certainly our lives were less driven by life insurance, club memberships and timeshare vacations. But as much as I needed my artistic community I could see its unspoken anxieties, its empire-building impulses, its rituals of self-congratulation. I was part of it.

At the same time, most of the happy people around me, I decided (perhaps somewhat unfairly), weren't particularly worthy of emulation. They were either shrilly effervescent or plain vapid. I didn't trust either. One seemed desperate, the other devoted to a life of sheep-like docility.

And then poems had gaps – those blank spaces on the page. And at one point, I fell headlong into one of those craters. That's when I experienced what aspiring verbal alchemists must also contend with: derailment. I now began to uncover vast, terrifying areas of myself that I could never hope to signpost in language.

There had to be another way.

My omnivorous reading of philosophy wasn't enough any longer. I was beginning to realize I couldn't live out my life in one sliver of my cerebral cortex. Or in one cranny of my left ventricle. It was clear to me now that I needed a way that wasn't a piecemeal engagement with mind or heart, but one that percolated into all of me. If I wanted to lead a less divided life, I had to start by accepting that I was lost.

And so, I turned seeker – conscious seeker, that is. I could deceive myself that I was learning from life. But most of the time I was trying not to make the same mistakes, and the rest of the time I was making them. I could tell myself I was being edgy and original when I was actually re-enacting age-old patterns of self-preservation.

I now found myself drawn to those who asked questions, who seemed to have confronted the terrors of a life evacuated of conferred meaning. They questioned the same things that the rest of us did, but seemed insane enough to stake their lives on a question mark. These crazy insurgents were the mystics of the world. And all of them seemed to be dead.

Enrolling for meditation and self-help programmes didn't boost my morale. If anything, it left me feeling a bit ridiculous.

Here I was succumbing to what I'd always abhorred – asking self-styled professionals for answers, after priding myself on being the independent upstart, the unlicensed seeker. And to be asking questions about the 'meaning of life' well into my thirties? It was mortifying.

But the questions gnawed. And they eventually ate a big hole into my life. So when I walked into a public talk by a person called Sadhguru at a south Mumbai auditorium in 2004, I'd already journeyed from being a determined amateur to a somewhat battered one – not ready to dissolve into a puddle of self-abnegation perhaps, but certainly willing to be surprised.

On meeting Sadhguru, he struck me as the first person I knew who combined intelligence with a palpable joy. And for all his knowledge of the self, he hadn't lost any of his capacity for wonder. That helped to banish the intermittent doubts I had along the way about his avowed state of self-realization.

Above all, his joy wasn't annoyingly monochromatic. He was capable of mystical insight and robust common sense. He could be wise and childlike, quiet and exuberant, profound and playful, meditative and impassioned, and I realized that none of these states were mutually exclusive. His knowledge of the inner life seemed inexhaustible, but his appetite for knowledge seemed limitless too. He was the only 'enlightened' person I knew, and yet he didn't act like he had arrived. He seemed to know about the nuts and bolts of the inner world, and yet he wasn't jaded. It was evident in the curiosity and aliveness he brought to every moment in his life.

He seemed to be proof that innocence and experience could go together. Or, to use another metaphor, that nirvana and samsara – or the Garden of Eden and the fallen world – were more fundamentally connected than I'd imagined. It wasn't that he was perfect. That would have been dull. He seemed – and this is the only word I could think of at the time – whole.

I realized that I didn't have to agree with him all the time. (On matters unrelated to the spiritual, we have had our disagreements, often heated, and those haven't abated.) It struck me that he wasn't looking for groupies. He wasn't looking for acolytes. In fact, he didn't seem to be looking, as far as I could see, for anything at all. His level of ease in his own skin intrigued me. Perhaps he *was* exactly what he was said to be: a free being?

Life around him has always been somewhat confusing. 'Rough and tumble' is how he once described himself as a guru. But it can also be a life of accelerated self-discovery. It's a bit like being in a car where he's at the wheel. Abandon and control, recklessness and accuracy, exhilaration and exactitude – as a hair-raising driver of cars and navigator of destinies, Sadhguru seems to embody all those contradictions in one crazy mix.

His advent in my life was cyclonic. In a poem I wrote at the time, I said it was like opening my coffee percolator only to find my roof flying off. As I emerged from the fear and exultation of that collapse, the winds blowing more gustily around me, I realized I could no longer live a life conveniently fragmented into daytime poet and surreptitious seeker. If I wanted to begin a journey towards wholeness myself, I had to accept my uncertainty, my rooflessness.

I could no longer live in worlds that seemed either barrenly secular or hermetically sacred. I needed betweenness. Bridges. Dual citizenship was suddenly a necessity – disruptive and often unnerving, but most reflective of what I now was.

The past twelve years with Sadhguru have been about realizing that there are other ways of 'knowing' than recourse to a book or to cerebral introspection. Being around a mystic has been about glimpsing deeper sources of nourishment, subtler methods of self-understanding, of journeying towards authenticity. To throw away the 'spiritual' because of my mistrust of phoney piety, I realized, was to throw away the baby with the bathwater.

Someone once informed me that I wasn't sceptical enough in my approach to Sadhguru. It gave me pause. Paradoxically, I suspect I am probably seen by some devotees as a far-from-model disciple: a little too angular, a little too irreverent. I've always thought I was quick to disagree, to argue, to cross-question, even when I know that Sadhguru's deepest answers are invariably non-verbal.

That was when I understood that scepticism, for me, isn't about blistering rationality. I value the freedom to doubt. But my doubts aren't banished by logic alone. I value the freedom to question. But I'm not looking for foolproof coherence, for hundred-watt illumination.

So no, I am not a sceptic if that means wanting a decoded universe. I know enough about poetry – and love – to know that the 'other' is best understood when embraced rather than anatomized. But I am a sceptic if that means feeling the need to ask questions that sometimes burn up my innards. The questions I ask Sadhguru are born of a feverish curiosity or gnawing anxiety, but often of plain wonder. And that wonder doesn't need a corseted sanity or prim reasonableness, cracked codes or solved riddles. It is at home with mystery.

I feel the need to reclaim more of that. Not a phoney innocence. Not a pseudo 'noble savagery'. Just the thrill of arriving again at the old realization that the world is 'magicked', and that you don't need to work very hard to make it that way.

And so, to Adiyogi.

This book is divided into three sections. In the first two sections, the voice is Sadhguru's. In Part One, he introduces us to Adiyogi and discusses his abiding fascination with this figure. The chapters here are interspersed with retellings of tales from the vast reservoir of Shiva legend and folklore.

In Part Two, Sadhguru turns fabulist, weaving a tapestry of narratives, yogic and mythic. As I recorded and pieced this together, it was difficult to know where the tradition ended and live spiritual stenography began. This is Sadhguru as raconteur and master, channel and spiritual guide all at once. The spine of this section is a yogic story, but this is punctuated once again with mythic tales embedded deep in the racial memory of the subcontinent.

I should point out right away that the demarcation between the 'magical' and 'logical' here is blurred – inevitably so. For differences notwithstanding, both the mythic and the yogic are rigorous and profound explorations, in their own way, of human subjectivity. Both entail their own brand of logic. Myth is enchantment, but rooted in profound existential truth. Yoga is a science, but a subjective science. Both are doorways. Both invite you to the same mysteries. Both are invitations to the beyond.

Much of Sadhguru's active life may be about affirming the importance of the 'yogic sciences' and 'inner engineering'. All very pragmatic. And yet, his approach to life is essentially non-utilitarian. Hear him tell a story and you know that you are in the presence of someone who takes the business of storytelling very seriously indeed. 'This is a culture that has always expressed truth in exuberantly imaginative and multilayered ways,' he often says. 'And that's what gives it its richness and colour. Each of these stories embodies a profound truth.'

When it's a story about Shiva, there is another charge to the storytelling altogether. Capable of moving from the personal to the impersonal, the prosaic to the poetic without a moment's warning, his take on Adiyogi can, at times, seem confusing.

But one thing is clear. Whether formless or embodied, celestial or terrestrial, mythic or historic, Shiva for him is *real*. Urgent, immediate, throbbingly present.

The final section of this book is devoted to discussions that explore this mystery. Since some of these dialogues unfolded on a journey to Mount Kailash, this section is an invitation to travel with a mystic. It is a chance to see a world, however blurrily, through his eyes. It is a chance to hear him speak about ideas and images in ways that confound the boundaries between the mundane and the mystical.

And then there is Adiyogi himself – remote and up close, legend and reality. For Sadhguru, Adiyogi is the ultimate. For me, Adiyogi has been more often than not just an excuse. An excuse to be around a living yogi and hear him talk about a being who distils every contradiction – life and death, the here and the hereafter, time and eternity – into a great, swirling present continuous.

In these conversations, I ask questions that I believe readers will share. Several are answered, some aren't. Some provoke only more questions. But it also felt right to leave some questions unanswered, shrouded in the kind of silence that often accompanies the presence of a mystic.

I believe these conversations address a single question I had to ask in multiple guises during the making of this book. It is a question I often asked in exasperation. It is a question that always received a different response – each time clearer and yet more tantalizingly mysterious.

It is a question I am still asking, though now in deepening fascination and incredulity: just *who* is Adiyogi?

PART ONE

ADIYOGI

SADHGURU

THE BEGINNING

Over fifteen thousand years ago, in the upper reaches of the Himalayas, where the snows are perennial and the skies terrestrial, a being appeared.

He was a being unlike anyone had ever seen – nine feet tall, ash-smeared, with flowing matted hair. Sometimes he sat absolutely still. At other times, he danced. His dancing was indescribable. Wild and ecstatic, it seemed to breathe exuberance into an entire universe. Planets and stars, rivers and forests, mountains and oceans exploded into life around him. When he was motionless, he seemed to become the ageless silence at the heart of all creation. He seemed to become life itself.

No one had ever seen anyone like him before. They did not know who he was, where he came from, what his origins were.

People gathered in huge numbers around him because his presence was quite extraordinary. It was clear that while he was on this planet, he was not of it. They waited, hoping for a miracle.

Nothing happened.

Much of the time, he just sat still, completely oblivious to what was going on around him. Except for a few tears of rapture that fell from his eyes, he showed no signs of life at all.

A tremendous miracle was happening before everyone's eyes, but they missed it completely. They could not see that his sitting still for days and months on end was the real miracle. They were expecting firecrackers. That did not happen. Everyone left.

Only seven men hung on. They could not leave. This mysterious being was no longer merely the centre of their worlds. He seemed like the kernel of the very universe, the key to all the mysteries of existence.

When he finally opened his eyes, they pleaded with him to share his experience with them. He dismissed them.

'This is not for people seeking entertainment. Go away,' he said.

But they persevered.

Many long years later, unable to ignore their unwavering commitment and radiant receptivity, Adiyogi – or the first yogi, as this being came to be called – relented. He directed his attention to these seven thirsty seekers and began expounding to them the nature of life.

It was on that full moon day – the first full moon after the summer solstice – that an entire exploration of the mechanics of life unfolded on this planet. It was on that day that Adiyogi became Adi Guru, the first Guru. That day is celebrated to this moment in the history of the Indian subcontinent as Guru Poornima.

What makes this day so important?

It was on this day that the seed of liberation was planted in the human consciousness. It was on this day that it was declared for the first time in human history that biology is not destiny, that it is possible for a human being to evolve *consciously*. The finite can turn infinite. The particular can turn universal. Compulsion can turn into consciousness. It is possible for a piece of creation to become one with the source of creation. The human creature can become a divine entity.

This insight did not give birth to faith. It instead gave birth to science. A science that aimed at making human beings the rulers of their own fate, the architects of their own destiny. Guru Poornima *predates* religion. It happened before the idea of religion even entered the human mind. The journey did not demand belief in a prescribed set of conclusions. The journey was about *exploration* – a fearless exploration of the profoundest depths of human consciousness. The ultimate aim was not God. The ultimate aim was liberation.

What Adiyogi transmitted to those seven disciples were the fundamentals of a science called *yoga* – union – a science of radical self-transformation that continues to live on thousands of years after that first exposition, a science that continues to empower human beings to blossom to their ultimate potential. The goal was *mukti* – freedom from a life of physical enslavement and psychological bondage. The goal was life itself – roaring, unfettered life. Ecstatic, boundless, infinite life.

And that freedom, Adiyogi declared, is within the reach of every human being.

A BIOGRAPHY OF EMPTINESS

In the yogic tradition, when we speak of Shiva, we could be alluding to either of *two* possibilities. We could be invoking Shi-va in the literal sense – as 'that which is not', a primordial emptiness. Or we could be invoking Shiva as Adiyogi, the first-ever yogi, the one who first perceived this emptiness.

This can often seem confusing. How can 'that which is not' and the first yogi be one and the same?

Let us look at it this way.

Yoga means 'union'. This means that *you cannot separate the one who perceives from that which is perceived*. Since the first yogi experienced the unity of existence, he has become one with 'that which is not'. He is one with Shi-va, the ultimate emptiness. The two are not separate any more. When I speak of Adiyogi, I travel seamlessly between these two definitions. I cannot separate the two because, in my experience, they are not separate.

The next section in this book tells the story of this larger-than-life yogi who walked the planet thousands of years ago. But before we plunge into that tale, let us rewind to an even more ancient story. The story of 'that which is not'. The biography of emptiness. The yogic creation myth.

Can ultimate emptiness really have a biography? And what do I mean by ultimate emptiness anyway?

This is not an exercise in metaphysical acrobatics. When I speak of 'that which is not', I am speaking of the existential – that which is the very basis of your life. It is a dimension that is always available, but most people are usually too busy or distracted to pay attention to it.

You could simply begin by looking up at the night sky. At first glance, you see the moon, that mysterious orb that has fascinated lovers, poets and mystics down the ages. You also see a blaze of stars – some radiant, some more dimly luminous. But if you continue to gaze upwards, what you gradually become aware of between that sprinkling of stars is just emptiness. An enormous expanse in which stars are just a small phenomena. Stars, suns, planets – these celestial bodies come and go. Entire solar systems and galaxies come and go. But that dark emptiness – that endures.

'That which is' is necessarily finite. But 'that which is not' can only be darkness. Light is produced because something is burning up. What is burning up can never be eternal. Whether it is a light bulb or the sun, both are sources of illumination with limited shelf lives. Both are burning up, and some day they will be over. It may take a hundred hours or a hundred billion years, but both will be over. In this existence, the only thing that is eternal is darkness.

So when you are a spiritual beginner, the divine is usually referred to as light. As you progress in yoga, we refer to the divine as darkness. And *that* is Shi-va – that interminability, that black infinitude.

Does that mean Shi-va is nothing?

No. Shi-va is *no-thing*. The hyphen is important.

Shi-va *is*. But Shi-va is not some*thing*. Shi-va is that which is not. Shi-va is that lap of vast no-thingness in which creation has happened. Over 99 per cent of the atom and the cosmos are, in fact, as we are told today, emptiness – simply no-thing. So, in the yogic tradition, when you utter the word 'Shi-va', it means that you

have ignited your own longing for no-thing. Or, to put it another
way, you have awakened to the unquenchable human thirst for that
which is beyond physicality. You have begun to seek that which is
beyond limits, beyond borders, beyond boundaries. That which is
beyond all definition.

'That which is not' comes into your focus only when you start
seeking your ultimate well-being. When you are seeking your
immediate well-being, 'that which is' is very important. This is the
familiar world of material phenomena – your body, your home, your
work, your relationships. When you begin seeking your *ultimate*
well-being, however, you are interested in a dimension beyond the
physical. Once questions of material well-being are addressed, it is
only natural for individuals to ask questions about their ultimate
well-being. This has happened with all the ancient cultures on this
planet. This is the natural progression of human enquiry.

In yoga, existence is divided into four dimensions: *sthoola*,
sooksbma, *shoonya* and *shi-va*. Sthoola means gross existence or
physicality. Everything that you can sense through the five sense
organs – everything that you can see, smell, taste, hear and touch
– is considered physical or sthoola. It is measurable, quantifiable,
verifiable. It can be analysed by your intellect, understood and
grasped.

But when existence goes beyond the empirical – that is, beyond
the perception of the five senses – and is still physical in nature, we
call it sookshma. Sookshma is a dimension that is still physical, but
cannot be grasped through the five senses. Nor can you analyse it
with your intellect.

Gnana means knowledge. If you are able to perceive the dimension
of subtlety beyond ordinary knowing, we call it *visheshagnana* or
vigyan, extra-ordinary knowledge. Vigyan is the ability to perceive
those dimensions which cannot be perceived through the five senses.
Today, science is entering those spaces. Nobody is ever going to see

a Higgs boson; they can only perceive its footprint. Today science is acknowledging the subtle realm of visheshagnana.

If you go even further, existence becomes shoonya – emptiness or the absence of form. There is no physicality here. Where there is no physicality, your sense organs and intellect become absolutely redundant.

If you go beyond shoonya, you reach the dimension of 'Shi-va' – absolute emptiness, the antithesis of everything that is. This dimension is non-physical, but it exists. It is the basis of all physical existence. When this dimension is personified, Shi-va becomes Shiva. In his ultimate state, Shiva is eternally still. One can only experience this state by stilling one's own existence.

When Shiva moves, his initial phase of movement is dark. He is therefore known as the Dark One. When he emerges and becomes a part of this world, he is light. If you want to transact with him, you deal with him as light. You can worship him, be devoted to him, seek his blessings.

This is the nature of every particle in existence. When it is still, it is dark. In the early stages of dynamism, it generates energy, but is still dark. Only when it moves at a certain speed does it become light. Anything that moves at the speed of light, as we know, becomes light.

But if you confront the dark face or go beyond that, you cannot transact with Shiva. If you want to go there, you need courage, you need to be willing to transcend, ready to leave everything you know. You need to be prepared to be sucked into another dimension altogether. No worship is possible there. There is just dissolution.

There one exists not as an accumulation of memory and experience, not as an embodiment of love or compassion. There one simply exists in an intensity of inclusiveness.

🔱

Modern science seems to be veering towards a similar understanding of the ultimate nature of existence. Both science and mysticism are, in fact, fuelled by the same spirit of wonder. Both are fuelled by the deep desire to know. Neither is about belief. So, they are, in essence, not so very different, and never have been. At one time, it seemed like they ran on parallel tracks. But recent convergences suggest that we could be on the verge of a new dialogue between the two.

Modern physicists have accepted that all existence is fundamentally energy. But now they also acknowledge that there is something else that they have no instrument to measure. They have begun to realize that there is a dimension of energy that seems to hold everything together. They recognize its existence, but have no clue to its nature. Since they are not able to perceive it, they call it 'dark energy'. For now they concede that it constitutes 73 per cent of the universe. (It will take time and evolution for them to see that it is, in fact, a lot more than that!) They also tell us that at the centre of our galaxy, and presumably of several others, is a 'black hole' which is constantly sucking creation in. At the centre of a black hole, they say, is a singularity, a place where creation and destruction happen simultaneously. In fact, scientists seem just one step short of saying: Shi-va!

In the yogic tradition, Shi-va is the unfathomable emptiness from which creation springs and into which it collapses. This is why traditional mythology personifies him as the Destroyer. At the same time, Shiva is Mahadeva, the greatest of divine beings, and the very Creator of this cosmos. An explanation for the process of creation *and* destruction is found in the very same figure.

Some years ago, I attended a presentation by an eminent physicist on the Big Bang Theory. I found it amusing because science is now beginning to sound just like yogic lore! Scientists even seem to be describing the same forms that yoga has always held as sacred.

Science today tells us that the universe is endless. Yogic culture talked of an ever-expanding universe millennia ago. It talks of the whole of existence as an eternal and ongoing dance between Shiva and Shakti. The non-physical dimension is Shi-va. The physical dimension of energy that animates the universe is Shakti. Shi-va is 'that which is not' and Shakti is 'that which is'. They are two aspects of the same reality.

Shi-va, the latent unmanifest dimension of reality, generates an energy called Shakti – an energy that is a consequence not of particles but emptiness, an energy without substance or basis. This energy ignites the void into a dynamic state of creation, maintenance and destruction. And thus emerges the entire realm of time and space, name and form, birth and death. From this begins the whole drama of life. Shi-va is the centripetal force that holds existence together; Shakti is the centrifugal force that gives rise to the explosive diversity of existence.

In yogic culture, we personified these ideas, infused plot and dialogue into existential insights and turned them into stories. There is a certain beauty to it, particularly because it means we found ways to talk about those dimensions that are beyond the realm of logic.

The story goes like this: Shiva, the Dark One, is in deep slumber. Since he is that which is nascent, that which is latent, Shiva can only be inert. So, he sleeps.

You could think of it like this. Imagine an impenetrable darkness. Allow that darkness to thin infinitesimally, and for the purposes of our story, imagine the vaguest silhouette of a being – a gigantic shadow of a primal being, containing all cosmic space within him, his wild locks splayed far over the universe, lying on his side, lost in an unimaginably profound slumber. Out of his navel emerges a flame of energy, fiery orange, somewhat feminine in nature. This twisty, serpentine shiver of energy – Shakti – shoots up high into the void, and since the only way it can function is to become one with him again, it bounces back, ricocheting deep into his heart.

This is a moment of union with far-reaching consequences.

For there now arises from the depths of this supine being, a roar. And out of his mouth erupts a fiery ellipsoidal form that stretches into infinity. This great blast of furious intensity – this primordial roar of creation – resounds into the farthest reaches of the cosmos. And this becomes the first form of Shiva. This is *Rudra* – literally, the one who roars.

As this first form – singular and undifferentiated – begins to reverberate, there is a spellbinding explosion of sound and light. Galaxies and planets, stars and moons, celestial realms and nether worlds, dimensions of the past and future, realms both subtle and gross, spew out of the mouth of Rudra, galvanized into life. This is the birth of plurality. Breathtaking plurality. Now begins the vibrancy and dynamism of physical creation.

This, in essence, is the yogic creation story.

Today, scientists speculate that the first form in the universe could have been ellipsoidal. Initially, this form could have been just one large roaring mass of gases. But gradually these hot gases expanded, cooled, became less dense, and gave rise to masses of creation; and that is possibly how the entire universe came into being about fourteen billion years ago.

Some physicists I have met concur that the alleged 'big bang' could well have been a series of bangs. In an automobile if you take off the manifold and start the engine, it would sound like a volley of bangs. But if you throttle it up, the engine roars. So, a series of bangs in close succession does, in fact, sound like a roar. And, therefore, the Big Bang of modern science and the Big Roar of the yogic perspective could be closer cosmological models than we might imagine!

As human beings, it is natural to think of the creation of life in terms of sexuality; so the first form in yogic lore was seen as a phallus, suggesting that Shiva was aroused and ready for creation. This primordial ellipsoidal form is known as the linga (which comes from the Sanskrit root word 'lina', and literally means 'form'). It is seen as the first form from which all other forms in the universe are said to have sprung. From inner experience, we know that the final form assumed by physical creation before it dissolves is also ellipsoidal. So the first and final forms are both lingas. The A and Z of creation, the alpha and omega of life, happen to have the same fundamental form.

When someone once asked me what this really meant, I told him that existence actually resembles a sandwich! When Shi-va, or no-thingness, took on form, it took on the shape of a linga. When creation dissolves, the final shape it assumes is also a linga. In short, the linga is the form at either end of creation, before and beyond which lies emptiness. Since it is a transitory phase, closest to the source of creation and dissolution, it is seen as a doorway – *a doorway to the beyond from both ends*. It is both form and an invitation to the formless.

It is only because a few human beings through history have found this passage that we realized that the ultimate nature of existence is boundless no-thingness. Otherwise we would have definitely imagined that the ultimate resembled a human being – maybe bigger and wiser and more capable than us, maybe gifted with a hundred heads or a thousand arms! But we would naturally think of the divine as a bigger and grander version of ourselves. It is because we found the passage through the linga that we realized that the nature of existence is actually infinite emptiness.

As a combination of male and female sexuality, the linga (which, in iconography, is always depicted as inseparable from the yoni or the womb) is an audacious symbol of divinity. In the hierarchy of instincts, sex is considered to be the lowest, and the desire for the divine the highest. But here divinity is represented by the metaphor of sexual union – a hugely courageous way of looking at life. Such an image would be impossible in a culture where perspectives of the sacred evolved out of narrow ideas of morality, good and bad, right and wrong. This is only possible in a culture where an understanding of the sacred evolved out of consciousness. There is no distinction between the sacred and the profane in this symbol.

With Shiva, nothing is, in fact, profane, nothing heretical, nothing taboo. Nothing is excluded, absolutely nothing beyond the limits of acceptability.

So what does this inspired symbol really signify?

If the masculine and feminine meet at the *mooladhara*, the lowest chakra or energy centre in the human system, that is sexuality. But if they meet within the highest chakra, the *sahasrara*, that is spirituality. That is the point at which the human meets the divine, the point at which creation begins and ends, the point at which birth and dissolution happen in endless simultaneity. *That* is self-realization.

In the yogic view, the masculine and feminine are seen as two fundamental qualities in existence. They have nothing to do with the biological condition of being male or female. As each one of us is a product of both father and mother, each individual is seen as a combination of the masculine and feminine in equal proportion. It is the dominance of expression that varies from person to person.

On the physical level, the sexual impulse is the creative force in existence. Sexual union denotes the biological propagation of human life. The body is created out of this. On the spiritual level, once again the same inner union of masculine and feminine is the source of all creation. It is the same energy. When it is dissipated on the level of the mooladhara, it is sex. When it moves to the sahasrara, the same energy becomes enlightenment. The sexual turns sacred. Animal nature turns divine. The human animal, *pashu*, turns into the Lord of Life, *Pashupati*. Exuberant, mutable nature, *Prakriti*, becomes one with the imperishable Absolute, *Purusha*. Creation becomes one with the source of creation. The two are now inseparable.

In tantric imagery, Shakti and Shiva are seen in terms of two chakras at either end of the human system. Shakti who lies coiled at the lowest chakra – the mooladhara – has a tremendous urge to ascend and meet Shiva. But he is inert; he will not come down. So she rises to meet him. The whole process of human evolution is to make this energy rise to the highest point, rather than get frittered away at the lower levels. Once Shakti and Shiva unite, the energy has reached its ultimate destination.

This is the supreme homecoming. The journey is complete. Nothing more remains to be achieved.

But the union is also annihilation. The birth of the infinite marks the dissolution (and dis-illusion) of the finite. This is why Shiva represents creation and the destruction of life as you know it. When your energies hit their peak, a new dimension of perception opens up, a dimension beyond all physical limitations. Now begins the downpour of another dimension – the dimension of the beyond.

In the yogic tradition, Shiva is referred to as *Kala*, the Dark One, and Shakti is referred to as *Kali*, his female counterpart. Of all of Shiva's manifestations, Kala is particularly significant.

For Kala is not just the endless darkness of space. Kala also means time. And so, the yogic sciences employ the same word for both time *and* space. This is because these are not seen as different.

Recently, scientists have recorded gravitational waves on the fabric of space–time. This confirms Einstein's theory that our experience of the physical world is relative. But this also reconfirms a time-honoured yogic insight: that time is the fundamental basis of creation.

One aspect of time relates to the physical nature of creation. Physical reality is cyclical: for example, a single rotation of the earth is a day, a revolution of the moon is a month, a revolution of the planet around the sun is a year. From the atomic to the cosmic, everything physical is always in cyclical motion. This is the aspect called Kala.

But there is an even more fundamental dimension of time that is beyond the cyclical. It is this ineffable dimension that holds the entire universe together. This is non-cyclical time, eternity, or what the yogic system termed *Mahakala*.

Let us look at it this way. Only in time, space is possible. Only because of space, form is possible, and all physical reality becomes possible. When Mahakala – a formidable dimension, potent with life – begins to reverberate, physical existence begins to dawn. Even gravity – the force that manages the time–space relationship and allows it to find expression – is seen as one small by-product of time.

Everywhere in the world the spiritual process is about transcending the physical world of form and returning to the realm of deathlessness, of eternity. Not because there is anything inherently wrong with the physical world. The problem is just that it is perishable, subject to cycles of birth and decay. The dark, dynamic aspect of Shiva has therefore been personified in mythology as *Kala Bhairava*, the Destroyer of Ignorance, he who annihilates the compulsive cycles of birth and death, being and non-being.

When Kala Bhairava – this vibrant state of darkness – becomes absolutely still, he returns to the eternal, fundamental Mahakala. When the last vestige of cyclical existence is annihilated, Mahakala is all that remains. This is the ultimate nature of existence, time beyond cycles, the dimension of time that endures when space has been annihilated, where everything is eternally here and now. This is the domain of raw, pulsating, unending life.

You can call it the Creator, or creation, or you can call it yourself

– it doesn't matter. This is the realm beyond 'this' or 'that', beyond 'you' and 'me', beyond 'here' and 'there', beyond 'yes' and 'no'. This is the domain of only 'yes' and 'yes'. This is Shiva.

For the ignorant, Shiva spells destruction. He is synonymous with a terrifyingly nihilistic view of the universe. This has given rise to several crude misconceptions about Eastern culture in the West.

There is even an unfortunate tradition in the Indian subcontinent right now which says that you should not keep an image of Shiva in your home. It is based on a rudimentary understanding of Shiva as Destroyer. The premise is that if you keep Shiva out, you could keep death at bay. As if that were even possible!

What Shiva dissolves are your delusions. He destroys only your psychological drama which lives on duality and fragmentation, separating you from the existential. This seductive drama seems real and compelling, even though it is entirely manufactured by you. This is what the ancients called *maya*.

Maya does not mean illusion, although it is often reductively interpreted as such. It simply means *our experience of life is relative*. Modern neuroscientists confirm this. It does not mean reality does not exist; it simply means that we are not seeing it the way it is.

This is why this tradition speaks so much of 'karma'. And this is why I often talk of the importance of 'responsibility'. For the very way you see, hear, smell, taste and touch the world is your responsibility; it is your karma; it is the destiny you have written for yourself, unconsciously. It is *your* doing. The spiritual process is about learning to write your destiny consciously. It means beginning the journey from the psychological – maya – to the existential – Shi-va.

And so, Shiva does not spell religion. Shiva spells responsibility – our ability to take our very life process in our hands.

When the old is destroyed, spirituality is not about filling up the empty space with a new set of beliefs. The aim of any authentic spirituality is never to convert you from one set of doctrines to another. The evacuated space – that you now see as emptiness – is tremendous intelligence. It is the intelligence from which the entire creation has sprung.

That space is life. That space is enlightenment. That space is whatever you choose to term the highest within you.

So, when you utter the word 'Shiva', you have actually articulated your own thirst for freedom. When you desire freedom, that is, in fact, what you mean: you want to destroy your limitations. You aspire to become unshackled, unlimited, unbound.

So, in a sense, it *is* true. Shiva should not be kept in your home. Shiva is not meant for those who are simply seeking a little more profit, a little more advantage out of life. Shiva is not meant for those who are trying to beat their loneliness in the company of God, or those aspiring for a place in paradise. Shiva is only meant for those whose greed is unlimited, for those who are not willing to settle for life in instalments, for those who want to become one with the very source of existence. If you go to the ultimate power in existence, you must also be going with the petition for the greatest possibility. You cannot be going with petty things to the big man!

From this perspective, it is useless to keep Shiva in your home. Locking him up in a room will not work because you cannot lock him up. If you have the courage, you carry him within you. If you are seeking the highest, you do not keep him in your home. You carry him in your heart.

How did yogis arrive at this understanding thousands of years before modern science?

Today, we believe the whole of existence has to oblige human logic – a tragically limited way to approach life. We think we can fit the whole of existence into our heads. But that is obviously impossible. Our logic can analyse the *physicality* of existence. But once we cross the physical threshold, logic is completely out of its depth.

If we try to understand the universe by going outward, knowing full well it is immeasurable, it is going to be an impossible project. We have no clue where this existence begins, where it ends, and where its centre is. It can only be an endless pursuit.

Yogic science took another route. It recognized that this little piece of life – the human being – is made the same way as the cosmos. It is made according to the same principles of creation. If you observe your interiority closely enough, you will know how a human being happened. Once you know that, you know, by inference, how *everything* happened.

Anyone can see this if they simply look within. If you cut a tree today, it is possible to look into the rings of the tree and talk about the past. It is possible to say when a drought happened in that land, when there was excessive rain, or a raging fire.

Similarly, if you pay attention to the human system with the needed awareness, you can find the very history of this creation inscribed there. Whatever has happened in existence is in some way recorded here, in this very body. If you look deep into yourself as a piece of energy, you can see that the information you carry goes all the way back to the beginnings of the evolutionary process that started with the single-celled animal, and even further back to the elements, the atoms, and then to the Big Bang and beyond. All the information – from that vast emptiness to matter, from the ape that you once were to the spiritual aspirant that you might have become today – is *right here* within this life that you consider to be yourself.

Whether you call it physics or spirituality, both of them are seeking the same thing: the basis of existence. One is trying to explore the outside universe and understand it. Another is trying to explore interiority and experience it. The fact that scientists are willing to spend billions of dollars just to *know* something – not necessarily for utilitarian purposes – sounds quite spiritual to me. But it doesn't have to cost that much!

This human being is just a reflection of creation. If you know the full depth and dimension of what it means to be human, you know everything that is happening out there. You cannot separate the two. In the same image as the creation is the Creator. That is why religions have said that the human being is created in the image of God. In yogic culture we just said, 'Everything that happened in this existence has happened in a small way within us.'

The Shiva within you has just gone into a long slumber. This is the only reason why he has not come into your experience. The deepest core within you is dormant. What is needed is an induction of energy to make that latency become awake again, as it happened at the very start of creation.

Once this core awakens and begins to dance with you, you realize the basis of yourself. You realize that you and 'that which is not' are not separate.

And so, Shiva is a dimension, a concept and a person. This is a unique and most significant aspect of this culture. What is the ultimate dimension is also *you*. It is not unattainable; it is something you can aspire for. *It is a beyond that is within your reach.* All you need do is seek it. It is your birthright.

'But what does that really mean?' I was once asked. 'It sounds puzzling. It sounds abstract. Can you explain what that is *really* like?'

I said it means Shiva is a bit like a packed lunch! You don't have to go to a restaurant to be served. You don't have to go to a temple or to heaven to find him. The ultimate nature of your existence always goes with you. There is only one place to go *and* it goes with you.

How's that for simplicity? You really cannot get a better deal!

WHEN SOURCE
BECOMES SYMBOL

There are multiple creation stories with Shiva as protagonist. It is important to remember that the Shiva here is not Adiyogi, the first yogi, but Shiva in his many mythic manifestations.

Why are there so many creation stories, so diverse and even contrary?

Because a single metaphor is never adequate to describe the mysteries of the universe. Here are three of them.

Lore tells such wild stories about Adiyogi that the so-called civilized world finds them difficult to accept. Modern-day listeners, ruled by logic, have eliminated these seemingly indigestible stories, often forgetting that this is where the essence of Adiyogi lies. Let us begin with a somewhat disconcerting creation myth.

It happened…

At the fountainhead of existence was the Great Mother – the source of all life. Through powers of self-generation, she gave birth to three sons: Brahma, Vishnu and Shiva.

In the course of time, she began to age. She now grew concerned because she saw that if she did not bear more children, the world would end with no more than these three. In her wisdom, she saw that this form of self-generation would not lead to a sturdy, long-term establishment of life on this planet. She realized the human tribe needed to be perpetuated through other means.

But there was no other man in the world. None except her three sons. If she had to choose a man, it had to be one of these three. So, she decided to do the unthinkable.

She approached Brahma and said, 'This is the only way to propagate our kind: you and I have to be together as man and woman.'

Brahma was horrified. 'Impossible!' he said. 'You are my mother. I cannot conceive of such a thought.'

The Mother was saddened, but not surprised. She went to Vishnu and made the same request, adding with some urgency: 'This is the only way for the world to continue. You must agree.'

Always known to be diplomatic, Vishnu did not respond as vehemently as Brahma. He just smiled and went away.

She now sought her last resort. She approached Shiva.

He listened and, without hesitation, did her bidding.

And that is how life in the world began.

That is Adiyogi, absolutely unidentified with his physical self. Impossible to digest, difficult to pigeonhole, he is everything that you don't really want but, at the same time, he is the very root of life. He cannot be contained within the framework of narrow logic. He is existence itself – raw, primal, untameable. And that is how the lore has been built. The aim is to destroy your limited ratiocinative mind and open you up to a different dimension of life altogether.

This myth also shatters ideas of duality and illuminates the singular nature of the source of creation. Whether the source is personified as male or female, god or goddess, is a matter of metaphor. Even if the material world is rooted in the dance of duality, the story reminds us that the source of creation is always unitary.

The second story offers a glimpse into the immensity to which we allude when we speak of Shiva – an inconceivable dimension well beyond the understanding not only of sages and philosophers, but of the gods as well.

It happened...

The Creator Brahma and the Preserver Vishnu came across a great pillar of fire. It seemed beginningless and endless, a column of vast unending effulgence. From this emanated the sound, Aum.

They gazed upon it for a long time, awed at its radiance and splendour.

Then they turned curious. They decided to investigate. They set out in search of its beginning and its end. Taking the form of a swan, Brahma rose high into the blue skies in pursuit of its summit. Taking the form of a boar, Vishnu burrowed his way deep into the darkest recesses of the universe in the hope of reaching its base.

Both failed. For this cosmic pillar was none other than Shiva himself, pristine and magnificent. To seek to measure the immeasurable is an act which only the human intellect with its irrepressible imperialist impulse is capable.

When Vishnu returned, he conceded defeat. However, not wanting to admit failure, Brahma boasted that he had, in fact, reached the summit. As proof, he presented a white flower. This, he claimed, was what he discovered at the roof of the universe. The white flower – the ketaki – vouched for the veracity of Brahma's claim.

The lie cost Brahma dear. For no sooner was the sentence uttered than Shiva appeared. The two gods paid him obeisance.

For this lie, Shiva declared, Brahma would henceforth be deprived of the privilege of worship. The flower, by agreeing to be accomplice to this subterfuge, fell from grace. Adiyogi refused to accept it as an offering henceforth. (However, an exception was made for the holy night of Mahashivaratri. To this day, the white ketaki flower is offered for worship only on this darkest night of the year, considered to be a night of profound spiritual possibility.)

Brahma's lie marks the first act of fundamentalism on the planet. The flower is punished for bearing witness and offering tacit support to the fundamentalist impulse. To claim a limited end to a limitless process, to reduce the infinite to the finite, to draw borders across the borderless, to make measurements of the unfathomable – this is the beginning of the human impulse to create certainty where none exists. It is the birth of pain, of suffering, of delusion.

The spiritual journey is a journey towards clarity, but never towards certainty. When you draw conclusions about beginnings and endings, you are a believer. When you accept that you really do not know anything, you become a seeker.

To be enlightened is not a condition of certainty. It is to move from limited knowing to boundless unknowing, from gravitas to grace. It is to awaken to a condition of borderless ignorance, of limitless uncertainty. When you are no longer bound by the limitations of creation, you are blessed with the freedom of the Creator.

The third story is a tale that reveals the many dimensions of Adiyogi – the androgynous cosmic being, Ardhanareeshwara, the roaring Rudra, the fearsome Bhairava, and the ever-compassionate Pashupati, Lord of Life.

It happened…

Before creation, Brahma, the cosmic creator, was asleep in Hiranyagarbha, a blue lotus on Vishnu's navel.

When he was fast asleep, there was no creation. The cosmos was a vast soup of emptiness. When the blue lotus unfurled, Brahma awoke. He wanted to create. He created the Prajapatis, the fathers of existence, and told them, 'Go out into the world and perpetuate.'

They asked, 'How do we do it?'

Then Brahma was at a loss. He did not know what to do. At that moment, a cosmic being, who was half man and half woman, appeared. This was Ardhanareeshwara whose left side was feminine and the right, masculine. When this being appeared, containing all dualities in a single body, Brahma realized the fault in his creation: he had created only one aspect of it. He had forgotten to create the feminine dimension.

He now created a woman. The first woman in existence was called Ushas. When Ushas came, desire arose. Brahma was infatuated by his own creation. Overpowered by lust, he lost control over himself and imposed himself on Ushas. She transformed herself into a cow to flee from him, but he turned into a bull and pursued her. She then turned into a mare, but he turned into a horse. She turned into a doe, but he became a deer. And so it went on. This is how all the life forms were created.

This indiscretion shocked Brahma's sons, the Prajapatis, the fathers of the world. They prayed that he be checked somehow in his terrible act of folly, but nobody dared stop the Creator.

Eventually, out of Brahma's own brow, a terrible being emerged and shot an arrow at the Creator. The arrow pinned him to the sky. The Prajapatis asked him, 'Who are you?'

He replied, 'I am Rudra.'

When Rudra pinned down Brahma, Brahma came to his senses. He bowed down to Rudra and thanked him for bringing him back to his senses. He also gave him the title Pashupati, or Lord of the Animals, recognizing that Adiyogi or Rudra is the lord or restrainer of all bestial passions within us. As a mark of gratitude, Brahma also gifted him a bull. This bull, Nandi, was hereafter Adiyogi's vehicle.

Now that Brahma had returned to his senses, he stopped his pursuit of Ushas. She dissolved. The same feminine principle would later become the divine embodiment of knowledge and intelligence, Saraswati. Initially, Brahma had objectified and dominated the feminine principle. Now, chastened and wiser, he took the new embodiment of the feminine principle as his consort, and she assumed the name of Saraswati, recognized as the Goddess of Wisdom, bringing intelligence and mutuality into the process of creation. Hereafter, they went about creating the whole of existence with much more responsibility and insight.

After some time, Brahma noticed that there was a certain restlessness in creation. He did not understand what was happening. Then

Saraswati told him, 'They are hungry; for creation to be nourished and to multiply, it needs to be fuelled.'

Brahma replied, 'Let these creatures eat each other and survive.'

Thus began the dance of predator and prey. So the animals that were capable of this started eating each other, but the gentler animals were hungry and at the mercy of the predatory aspects of creation. They had nothing to eat, so they turned to Pashupati and begged him, 'We have nothing to eat, and we live at the mercy of other animals. Help us.'

So, Adiyogi went into deep meditation. The heat of his penance created all the herbs, shrubs, trees and creepers on this planet. Because he created all the vegetation, he became the master of flora. He came to be known as Vrikshanatha, Lord of the Trees.

Now, the herbivorous animals ate the plants, and life continued. But Brahma had another question: 'On what will these plants survive?'

Adiyogi replied, 'On the five elements, the pancha bhutas.' Because he provided the five elements for the plants to survive, he came to be called Bhuteshwara and Bhutanatha, lord or master of the five elements, or Bhutesha, embodiment of the five elements.

After some time, Brahma found that the animals were eating, reproducing and multiplying so rapidly that the cosmos was teeming with life. Though existence can be created on a whim, to nurture and bring it to fulfilment, a more profound approach is needed. Brahma had the power to create, but he did not possess the wisdom to sustain and guide his creations. As the world grew crowded, he grew perplexed.

Saraswati said, 'You forgot to create death. Every entry has to be balanced with an exit. If all beings just remain here, there is no meaning to life. You must create death.'

So Brahma created Mrityu, the Goddess of Death, an exquisite maiden in red robes. He summoned her and said, 'You must go and kill.'

She was horrified at the role that had been assigned to her and asked, 'Why should I kill?'

Brahma said, 'Life means nothing unless there is death. So you must kill.'

But Mrityu was not convinced. Adiyogi found her in a desolate place, weeping, and he consoled her. 'Don't worry. You go ahead and perform the role assigned to you. I will make sure that every life form that you kill is born again. So although you are a destroyer, your role will still be that of a nurturer, a mother.'

And so, Mrityu established herself as Mahakali and Adiyogi established himself as Mahakala, the Lord of Time. Thus, the sediment of destruction becomes the foundation of a new creation, making him the guardian of birth and death, the master of time. Though Brahma started the process of creation, it is Adiyogi who stabilized it and ensured its perpetuation. That is why he is known as Kalpeshwara and Kalpanath, or lord and master of creation, or Kalpesha, the embodiment of creation.

When Adiyogi looked at this cycle of creation and the nature of human death, disease, frustration, pain and suffering, he became deeply miserable. He could not understand the point of such a creation.

But Brahma, on the other hand, was very proud of this creation. He sprouted four heads to view all four sides of creation. In his hubris, he even sprouted one extra head, looking up at the skies. Adiyogi could not stand the Creator's arrogance. He turned into Bhairava, the fierce one, and plucked off Brahma's fifth head and ripped it apart. Brahma's folly was to turn the existential into the psychological, to raise a barrier between creation and the creator. He forgot that to be able to create is a privilege in itself. To derive pride from creation is to fashion a false layer of separation between the two.

Howling in pain, Brahma begged for mercy. Then Bhairava said, 'You have created a world which is illusory, ridden with unnecessary pain and suffering. And so, although you are the creator, nobody will worship or celebrate you in this world in any way.'

Tainted with Brahma's blood, Adiyogi went and sat in a place called Avimukta in the city of Kashi. He brooded for a long time in great pain. He asked Brahma, 'Why did you create all this torment and suffering?'

Brahma said, 'I just created the world. It is neither beautiful nor ugly. It is neither enjoyable nor tormenting. It is simply there. It all depends on what you choose to do with it. If you get caught up with the delusions of the mind, this is the way it is. If you use the mind to reach enlightenment, then you are beyond this. It is all up to the individual.'

Adiyogi said, 'But you created the mind too, which is the source of all trouble.'

Brahma replied, 'What you do with the mind is up to you. The choice is yours.'

Then Adiyogi sat down to think about how to transcend the mind, how to transcend the cycles of samsara, the whole process of life and death. After many years of profound meditation, he came up with a solution. What he propounded was a way to go beyond the bondage of life, a method of yoking oneself to the unlimited rather than the limited. Every being who was frustrated with life assembled to hear the great teacher. Gods, sages, ghosts, ghouls and goblins, everyone assembled. His concern was not just for human life but for all forms of life, from a serpent to a sage.

On the darkest night of the year, which later came to be called Mahashivaratri, he sat and expounded how everyone could transcend the painful cycles of existence. His listeners could grasp some parts of his discourse, but no one could imbibe all of it. Everybody found small paths to laughter, joy and peace, but nobody found the ultimate and eternal way.

Seeing the terrible power of delusion to hold people in its thrall, Adiyogi withdrew to the harsh, unapproachable terrain of the upper Himalayas and went into a profound state of stillness. He now divined multiple ways of reaching ultimate freedom for those rooted in the limitations of the physical form. As for those beyond the physical, he revealed numberless ways. Over aeons he incubated and refined these methods into 112 different ones, through which there could be an ultimate solution for every living being.

This is the reason why those on the path of yoga are associated with Adiyogi. For, on that day when Adiyogi turned south and became Dakshinamurti, the teacher who faces south, he gave the world the yogic science, the complete path to immediate and ultimate well-being, a path of unbounded ecstasy and liberation.

THE ETERNAL OUTLAW

A few years ago, when I was interviewed by an American magazine, I was asked, 'Who is the most significant person in the West to have worked for human consciousness?'

Without hesitation, I replied, 'Charles Darwin.'

The journalist said, 'But Charles Darwin is a biologist!'

I said, 'Yes, but he was the first to tell people in this part of the world that it is possible to *evolve*, that life can move from one dimension of existence to another.'

Charles Darwin talked of biological evolution about a century and a half ago in the West. Adiyogi, the first yogi (as distinct from the Shiva of myth and legend), explored a parallel line of enquiry almost fifteen thousand years ago in the East.

According to the trajectory explored by Adiyogi, the earliest forms of life were aquatic. Later, they turned amphibious and then terrestrial. Gradually, beings emerged that were half man–half animal, who morphed in time into dwarf-like human beings. When the first full-fledged human beings came forth, they were ruled by volatile impulses and emotions. Later, they learnt to restrain their tempestuous instinctual and emotional lives, and grew more stable and equanimous. In the next stage, they learnt to transmute their primal urges and emotions into sweetness and ecstasy. Still later, they transcended this unconscious world of impulses and emotions altogether and turned meditative. The human being of the future, said Adiyogi, will be a fully conscious, extraordinarily capable being, endowed with the ability to explore the deepest mysteries of the universe.

Thus, the ten stages that he delineated offered not merely a biological but an existential template. This was later absorbed into the popular religious culture of the subcontinent as the ten avatars or manifestations of life.

Unlike biological evolution, which happens over time without our conscious participation, spiritual evolution can happen much more rapidly, Adiyogi asserted, if it is undertaken consciously. All it takes is willingness.

Down the centuries, mystics have explored fragments of human consciousness. They have found one doorway here, one doorway there. But nobody has explored *every possible doorway to human consciousness*. No one did it before Adiyogi. And no one has needed to do it since. His work remains alive for those who have the eyes to see it.

His work began over nearly fifteen thousand years ago and, centuries later, it is still alive. You cannot kill it. He was the first to propound that we could use each and every point in our body as a pathway to freedom. His legacy is not a single method. He offered, instead, a mind-boggling plurality of ways to reach the ultimate.

Nothing was excluded. And no one was excluded. This prodigious system of self-knowing offered a path for everyone – people of all backgrounds and persuasions, of every cultural, social, moral, ethical and ideological context. That makes him the ultimate spiritual democrat.

He was also the first to expound spirituality as a science, not a faith (for this exposition occurred prior to the birth of religion); as a tool, not a tenet; as a device, not a dogma.

Historically, there is evidence to suggest that the primary divinity worshipped in the Indian subcontinent was 'Rudra'. Rudra was also referred to as Shiva or Adiyogi and the inhabitants of this land gave him an endless litany of names and forms. The oldest piece of iconography that depicts him is probably over 4,500 years old. It is a seal of a three-faced man seated in siddhasana, a yogic posture, wearing a horned headdress, with a bull and several animals around him.

As a protagonist in mythic lore, he is definitely older. This lore invokes him in a richly symbolic language. It is easy to trivialize this coded imagery. It is possible to approach it in a spirit of naïve literalism. It is also possible to see it as the product of an overheated imagination. But that does it no justice. We will unpack this imagery later in this book.

For now, it is enough to acknowledge that the picture is a colourful one. We are told that Shiva wore a crescent moon on his head. That he adorned himself with a snake. That he was clad in animal skin. That he was smeared with ash. That he was creator of the universe and dancer of ultimate devastation, all at once.

Between legend and archaeology, between poster art and myth, a complex portrait emerges.

In the tradition, he is terrible one moment, beautiful the next, compassionate one moment, ferocious the next. He is an ascetic and, at the same time, an ideal householder. He is a great yogi and, at the same time, an utterly intoxicated dancer. He is everything that life can be. He is not even regarded as a god. He is called Mahadeva. The word 'deva' means a divine being. Anyone who is not mired in the physicality of life is considered a divine being in the East. The name indicates that he was considered the greatest of all divine beings.

For every statement we make about Adiyogi, the reverse is also true. This was a being who assumed all kinds of forms and states because he refused to limit himself to any particular dimension. His whole persona has been manufactured in such a way that everything in existence can be fitted into his character. That is why he has a million names and yet, ultimately, is nothing. Because he is nothing, we can call him anything we please.

The many forms of Adiyogi have been intentionally crafted so that you cannot digest him easily. He has a snake around his neck. He wears a garland of skulls. He is the most uncivilized being, and yet has such a powerful radiance around him that you cannot stay away from him. There is a helpless attraction and a powerful repulsion at the same time. The whole idea behind fashioning such an image – that embodies life and death all at once – is to make the point that whatever you call divine is something that can never be logically understood. It can be experienced, but never grasped.

There is a deep science at work here. He is given this kind of impossible character because if you can accept him, you can accept everyone in the world. If you can accept Adiyogi, you have, in fact, accepted all of existence in one stroke.

You can call him anything you please. He has innumerable forms and manifestations. There is a distant, enigmatic, non-perceivable godhead that we call Ishwara; a benevolent personal god that we call Shambho; an uncomplicated hermit or endearingly naïve, easy-to-please Bhola; the wise master and fountainhead of the world's greatest wisdom traditions, Dakshinamurti; the dynamic dancer and source of all creativity, Nataraja; the fierce destroyer of ignorance, Kala Bhairava; the enchanting seducer, Somasundara, which means more beautiful than the moon; the lord of the five elements, Bhuteshwara; the easily forgiving Ashutosh; the absolutely and utterly still ascetic Achaleshwara.

You can make him hideous, you can make him beautiful. Many times he was a yogi who just sat unmoving. Many times he was a mad, dancing drunk. Nothing is strange to him, nothing is foreign to him. Everything is part of him for he explored every aspect of life. The problem was just that he was a little too inebriated to market himself!

Why do I invoke Adiyogi so recurrently? It is a question I am often asked. The answer to that is simple.

It is not because I want to anthropomorphize the divine. It is not because I want to introduce some devious mode of pagan worship. It is not because I want to usher in some new Eastern cult.

I invoke him simply because he is vital for our times.

And he is vital because there is nothing more important in the world right now than raising human consciousness. We have the tools and technologies in our hands with which we can make this world a paradise, or turn it into a living hell, or obliterate it altogether because of our own capabilities. In other words, we have reached a point where if we do not raise human consciousness, our intelligence and capability is going to work against us. We are racing rapidly towards self-sabotage.

It is not the uneducated who are threatening the life of this planet today; it is those who are educated, technologically capable and who consider themselves civilized who are doing the necessary work of uprooting all of humanity and the world. We have enough nuclear weaponry today to destroy this planet many times over.

We also have an economic engine that we are desperately trying to drive at a faster pace. We know it spells destruction. But we are in a compulsive mode, and cannot stop the momentum. We really do not need another nuclear explosion to annihilate life on this planet. Just a successful economy can do it quite effectively!

How did we get ourselves into this mess?

We got here because we developed our intellect at the expense of our interiority. We made the mistake of believing that the intellect was synonymous with our entire mentalscape. Right now, we use the single faculty of the intellect and mistake it for everything, forgetting that the mind is much more than that. The Eastern culture spoke, in fact, of sixteen faculties of the mind of which the intellect is only one. It divided these into four basic categories: the discerning dimension or intellect (*buddhi*); the accumulative aspect or memory (*manas*); the identity aspect (*ahankara*); and awareness (*chitta*), which is beyond both intellect and memory.

The intellect has received enough bad press. It is routinely disparaged by religious traditions. It is not my intention to add to that disparagement. The intellect is not the problem. It has, in fact, contributed hugely to human culture and civilization. It is a wonderful tool – a scalpel that can cut through any object, an incredible instrument for discernment, dissection and analysis, crucial to human survival.

The problem is that the intellect has assumed disproportionate importance. We have shackled it to our identity, ahankara. Once the intellect is identified – with gender, class, culture or race – it is no longer a useful tool. It is like using a sticky knife: if you cut onions with a knife and use the same sticky knife to cut cake the next day, everything will taste like onions!

An identified intellect leaves you with a completely distorted experience of reality. The human struggle is just this: you are unwilling to shake off the bits and pieces of knowledge you have acquired because these give you some sense of security and identity. For a tiny bit of knowledge, you are giving up the cosmos!

Additionally, in isolation from other faculties of the mind, the intellect is a disaster. For while the other dimensions of the mind enhance, the intellect can only divide. It does not allow you to simply *be* with anything completely.

As a human being, you are just an infinitesimal extension of this planet – and not even a separate extension! Even now, you have to breathe, you have to eat, you have to drink – you are constantly connected to the rest of existence. Without this ongoing transaction you could not exist for a moment. You are a mere pop-up and one day you will pop out. The body knows that. But the intellect chooses not to. It cuts you off from this reality and gives you a virtual identity that doesn't really exist. This is what the tradition called 'maya' – a make-believe world, a state of self-delusion.

When you go by the intellect alone, you dissect. But the nature of consciousness is *inclusion*. Consciousness is one big embrace of the universe. If that experience does not happen to an empowered intellect, that intellect is going to destroy the world. In the East, there are several proverbs that say that when people show symptoms of an overactive intellect, they are heading towards total destruction.

Take the example of the human family. There was a time when a hundred or more people could live together as one unit. Over time, it came down to four. Now often even partners have to live separately! There is nothing intrinsically right or wrong about this. It is just symptomatic of the growing significance of the intellectual dimension in modern life: it is essentially divisive. And if you go further, you will become schizophrenic, because the intellect will also divide the self into different parts! In today's world, there is much effort towards unity, intellectually trying to put everything together. But *if you try to stitch the world together with a knife, it will only leave everything in tatters.*

So, the crucial ingredient missing in the world today is what yoga calls chitta – the deepest dimension of the mind, intelligence unsullied by memory, which connects you to the very basis of creation. Chitta is awareness. Awareness is not alertness; it is aliveness; it is a profound intelligence that lies beyond the intellect, beyond memory, beyond judgement, beyond karma, beyond all divisions. It is the intelligence of existence itself, *the very cosmos in the living mind.* In the yogic tradition, it is said that once you distance yourself from the compulsions of your genetic and karmic software, as well as the vested interests and identifications of your intellect, you are in touch with chitta, an unclouded consciousness.

Now, your life returns to the way it was always intended to be – radiantly alive, fresh, immaculate. Even the divine has no choice but to serve you. You have now enslaved Shiva!

Adiyogi becomes hugely significant in such a context because in this area there is no one on this planet who has explored and revealed as much as he has. In terms of creating the most extensive and sophisticated system of human self-understanding – 112 methods by which human beings can explore and reach their fullest potential – there is no one whose contribution exceeds his.

Adiyogi knew life by becoming one with it – not cerebrally, but experientially. A yogi is one who has experienced union with the whole of existence. What Adiyogi represents, therefore, is *knowing*, not knowledge. Knowledge is intellectual accumulation; it is information gathered and processed in bits and pieces. Knowing, on the other hand, is neither intellectual nor accumulative.

If you pass by a flowering plant and you know the chemistry of its fragrance, that is one dimension of knowledge. If you know the experience and ecstasy of that fragrance, that is another dimension of knowledge. But if you *become* the fragrance, that is knowing. That is also aliveness.

A knowing that is hundred per cent experiential. A hundred per cent alive. A hundred per cent here and now. This is what Adiyogi represents. And that is why despite multiple attempts to appropriate him, he cannot be domesticated by any sect or scripture, dogma or doctrine.

Nature has set some laws for human beings. Breaking through the cyclical laws of physical nature is the basis of the spiritual process that Adiyogi explored. In that sense, yoga is a science for those who seek to be outlaws. And that is what Adiyogi represents: the ultimate outlaw.

It happened…

A line had formed at the entrance of the gates of heaven. St Peter was opening the account books and inspecting each person. Then the turn came of one man in a loud flowery shirt and leather jacket, smoking a cigarette. Behind him was a priest from St Mary's, Alabama. The priest could not believe that a man like this had the gumption to stand in a queue to enter heaven, and that too, ahead of him.

When the man's turn came, St Peter asked, 'Who are you?'

The man said, 'I'm Joe Luigiani, taxi driver from Las Vegas.'

The priest from Alabama who was standing behind him thought, 'Oh my god, from the Sin City, and that too, an Italian!'

Then St Peter opened his book and said, 'Oh, you have done really well.'

He took out a silk robe with gold brocade and gave it to him to wear. Then he clapped his hands and two angels appeared.

He said to them, 'Please escort him to his quarters.'

So with two ethereal angels on either side, wearing the silk robe with gold brocade, Joe Luigiani walked away into heaven.

The priest couldn't believe this. 'This taxi driver from Sin City! And on top of it, an Italian!'

Then his turn came.

'Who are you?' St Peter asked.

He said, 'I am a priest from St Mary's, Alabama. I have been in the service of God for forty years.'

St Peter opened the book and looked at it. Then he gave the priest a rough workman's clothes, handed him a mop and said, 'You can continue in the service of God.'

The priest said, 'Hey, wait a minute. Just now I saw that Italian taxi driver from Sin City getting treatment like that, and I have to mop the floors in heaven!'

Then St Peter said, 'See, here we go by the results. The manner of your preaching made people sleep. The manner of his driving made people pray – even in Sin City.'

In yoga, too, we go by the results! Adiyogi was the first to establish that unless you do the right things, the right things will not happen to you, thus moving us from unrealistic expectations to conscious choice, from passive worship to dynamic responsibility.

I am often asked, 'Are you a devotee of Adiyogi?'

I am most definitely not. I do not see Adiyogi as a god, but as a being who bequeathed to this world the most incredible spectrum of tools for self-transformation. I often joke that he is my fifty per cent partner. He's the silent partner; I'm the working partner. Without his investment, I cannot run the show; without me, at this point in time, it isn't easy for him to find expression in the world. So, it's a deal!

I did not willingly take on this partnership. It was a forceful imposition – but what a blessed imposition! He destroyed the smart man that I believed I was, and awakened me to an intelligence far beyond my intellect. As I once wrote in a poem, 'I would have it no other way'. I wouldn't trade this blissful state of ignorance for *any* other condition.

I did not woo him. It is just that somehow that which is referred to as Adiyogi or Shiva got mixed up with my breath. I did everything possible to shake him off, but I failed. I gave in because there was no alternative!

I have never sought Shiva temples, never performed any form of ritual or worship. I have never prayed in my entire life. I have not studied a single scripture. The profoundest literature I have ever read is probably an *Asterix* comic! Shiva was never my wish or my longing. It is just that if you clear space within yourself, if you dismantle your personality, you will discover that which is called Shiva as the fundamental basis of your being. The logic is simple: if you do the right things, the right things will happen to you even without your intent.

Shiva is not one more idol to beg to for a better deal. If you empty what you think of as yourself, Shiva *is*. You can call that by any name or form, or if you have the awareness, you can look at it as formless energy or limitless non-being. But that which contains everything – or 'that which is not' – is Shiva.

In every generation, a few yogis have emerged. If they happened to surface in the Indian subcontinent, people have sometimes referred to them as incarnations of Adiyogi. But nobody has ever *claimed* to be an incarnation of him. His knowing was of such magnitude that most yogis see themselves as no more than a single strand of hair in the wild abundance of his matted locks.

There is nothing I can do without him. Though I have a reputation for being ruthlessly logical, my every action, my every breath, exudes him. He is so much a part of my life and my being that everything that I do, in one way or the other, comes from that source.

Ever since my perception opened up to life beyond my five senses at the age of twenty-five, there was only one goal in my life: to fulfil the vision of my guru. When I speak of my guru, I speak of a yogi who appeared before me three lifetimes ago at a crucial moment of my spiritual growth.

I was referred to as Shivayogi in that lifetime. I had already lived out two lifetimes of intense and fruitless spiritual practice. My guru appeared and made the ultimate happen for me with just a touch of his staff.

My experience told me, 'This is it.' But I was a devotee of Adiyogi then, and my mind was trained to believe that unless Adiyogi appears, this cannot be real. Everything that needed to be realized had been realized, but there was still the residual impression of two lifetimes which said that unless grace comes in the form of Shiva, it is not complete.

So, out of his compassion, my magnificent guru, Sri Palani Swami, appeared before me as Adiyogi. He took that form just to satisfy that impression within me. It was only then that I could accept him. Since that moment, whatever I have done is in service of Adiyogi and an expression of his will. I see no difference between him and my master.

When Adiyogi awakens from his dormant state and comes alive within you, life is a constant eruption of energy. Every single moment is explosive. It makes everything else seem trivial – a bit like playing marbles. You play with marbles, but whether you win or lose doesn't decide the quality of your life. Now just sitting still is enough. Nothing more needs to happen.

That is how it has been for me since that moment. If I simply sit and close my eyes, I could sit until I fall dead, because what is happening within me is more incredible than I can ever describe. Whether something in the outer world happens the way I want makes no real difference to me because what is happening inside me is so enormous.

It is because I know the depth and the dimension of Adiyogi's work that I know he has not found even a fraction of the acknowledgement that he deserves. Deep within me is an ache that has grown over the years because I know we have not done him justice.

For what he has contributed to the human race, for having offered the fundamental nourishment for every spiritual movement that has ever arisen, he has definitely not found enough recognition. The dimension of knowing that he imparted has been the spine of knowing for the whole world. It is this spine of knowing that still feeds the essential spiritual process on this planet.

Externally, my life is dynamic. I am engaged in a huge volume of activity: there are health care, social, educational and environmental initiatives, in addition to spiritual programmes, for which I travel all over the world. And yet, I would consider all this to represent just *one per cent* of my life.

My real work is to allow Adiyogi to find expression in this world. Just this. Nothing else.

The first yogi on this planet. One who delved into creation and emerged as the source of creation. How are we to understand this phenomenon? Is this the realm of fact? Or is this a fairy tale?

The culture of the Indian subcontinent has always presented reality in the form of stories, recognizing that stories embody deeper truths than mere records of historical facts. Many of these fantastic legends, therefore, represent profound insights.

None of what I know of Adiyogi's own life contradicts the lore. But as a yogi, I do know the deeper mysteries to which the lore points. What unfolds in the next section is a story and a science, a tale and a technology. This is the realm where science turns subjective, where fact and fable, poetry and profundity, magic and logic become inextricable.

Welcome to the realm of the mystic.

THE KAILASH OF THE SOUTH

*The Velliangiri Mountains in southern India have been the abode of
countless seers and sages down the ages. These are not mere mountains.
They are a cascade of energy, a torrent of grace.*

*My allegiance to these mountains goes back many lifetimes. For me
there is no sacred geography on the planet that surpasses this.*

*These mountains are referred to in the southern yogic tradition as the
Kailash of the South. This is because Adiyogi walked here. Although
he lived in the Himalayas, legend tells us he did come down south at
one point in his life.*

It happened…

*Punyakshi, a woman of extraordinary spiritual capability and
perception, lived in southern India. She was a woman of such power
that she was regarded by society as an oracle with immense insight. She
developed a deep passion for Adiyogi and resolved to marry none but
him.*

*In the distant Himalayas, Adiyogi was moved by her devotion. But
the society around Punyakshi grew concerned because they believed
that if this union was consummated, they would lose her and she would
no longer be able to guide her people. So, the people around her did
everything possible to thwart her dream.*

But Punyakshi was determined, and Adiyogi responded with equal ardour. The wedding date was fixed.

This alarmed her people even further. They tried every means at their disposal to sabotage these plans. First, they appealed to Adiyogi: 'If you marry her, we will lose the guidance that her powers of perception offer us.'

Adiyogi was unmoved. He continued to prepare for the wedding. They tried again. They said, 'If you want this girl as your bride, there are a few conditions. You have to pay a bride price.'

Adiyogi said, 'What is the bride price? I am willing to pay anything.'

So, they said, 'The bride price is this: a sprig of sugarcane without rings, a betel leaf without veins, and a coconut without eyes.'

It was an impossible bride price because it demanded the unnatural – a sure-fire way of preventing the wedding.

But Adiyogi tapped into his immense occult capabilities and created these objects. In this romantic and passionate mode, he was willing to break all rules. And so, he violated the fundamental laws of nature to meet the demands of this unjust bride price. He then started proceeding south towards the wedding.

In desperation, Punyakshi's people placed one more condition. 'You must be married before the cock crows tomorrow morning. If you are not married before sunrise, the wedding cannot happen.'

So, Adiyogi accelerated his pace, determined to reach on time. Punyakshi, in the meantime, was making all the preparations for a grand wedding.

The leaders of society saw that Adiyogi was effortlessly dispensing with all the obstacles they had set for him. It looked like his promise to this woman would be fulfilled. They were now about to lose the precious eye of intuition that was their prized possession.

So, on the morning of the wedding, they conspired to make the rooster crow earlier than usual. They heaped up a large hill of camphor and set fire to it. Seeing the illumination, the cock crowed before sunrise.

Seeing the light and hearing the rooster on his journey southward, Adiyogi knew that his beloved Punyakshi would believe he had failed her. He froze in his tracks. Shattered that he had failed to keep his word to his most cherished devotee, he sank to the ground. (The place where Adiyogi sat, dejected at having failed his would-be bride, is believed to be the temple town of Suchindram in the state of Tamil Nadu.)

On hearing the cock crow, Punyakshi was furious that her lover had failed to keep his word. She tore down all the wedding preparations, kicked and broke all the pots laden with food for the celebration. In a fever of rage and grief, she went to the southernmost edge of the land and stood there, looking out at the ocean. She stands there to this very day as Kanyakumari – the heartbroken goddess frozen in eternal wait for her divine lover.

And so, society managed to foil the plans of Adiyogi, an extraordinary being of extraordinary powers. This childlike innocence has been his legendary trait. The intelligence that he represents is not street-smartness or worldly wisdom; his is the profound intelligence that makes life happen. Adiyogi is a classic embodiment of this contradiction: the epitome of ultimate perception and a chosen vulnerability, all at once. This is why he is known as Bhola or Bholenath, the one who is easily deceived. He chooses to be this way. This has been the voluntary condition of many yogis down the centuries.

Although he knows the beginning and end of the drama of life, Adiyogi still plays the game. Although a man of perception, he still participates with endearing exuberance and wholehearted involvement in the charade of samsara.

And so, for his failure to fulfil his beloved's desire, Adiyogi drove himself into a state of despondence. In such a state, it is said he went up to the very summit of the Velliangiri Mountains and sat there for a length of time. To this day, these mountains carry a different energy. This is because Adiyogi did not sit here in blissful meditation; he sat there, deeply disturbed and despondent. This despair gradually changed to rage – a great rage without purpose and direction, a rage that sprang from having succumbed to one's limitations, a rage that grew in time into an oceanic energy capable of engulfing all limitations and rendering one to the ultimate.

In the tradition, wherever Adiyogi stayed for a certain length of time was referred to as Kailash. That is how these mountains came to be known as the Kailash of the South. Because he lived here for a time and invested the place with a certain kind of energy, a number of yogis followed suit. So down the ages, for thousands of years, there is a history of seers who have been associated with this region. They came to be called siddhas – siddhars in Tamil – and evolved a unique system of mysticism that lives to this very day.

When Adiyogi sat on this mountain, it was not in a benign mode. It was in a state of ferocious intensity. This intensity is a tremendous possibility. But very few human beings ever come in touch with it. If they do, very rarely do they find social acceptance to deliver it to the world. Most people want the soft divine; they cannot handle such an intense, high-voltage form.

When the yogis of the Velliangiris came down from the mountains in the past, they spoke of Adiyogi as 'Shambho'. Different yogic systems have created various forms of Adiyogi. These were created by those who had absolute mastery over their systems and their energies. They created very beautiful and very hideous forms. Shambho is one of the more auspicious ones. He is a very gentle form of Adiyogi, which is rare. Shiva is usually wild. But by invoking Shambho, the yogis of this region tried to soften and temper the intense energies of these mountains so that they would work in the world.

Fundamentally, Shambho means 'the auspicious one'. Traditionally, the two words 'Shiva Shambho' are uttered together. This is because Shi-va – 'that which is not' – is also the most auspicious. You can find fault with 'that which is'. You can like it or dislike it; you can agree with it or disagree with it! But 'that which is not' is perfect. 'That which is not' is the most auspicious, because nobody can find fault with it. And so, Shiva is considered an emblem of destruction — not because he is out to destroy you, but because he is already destroyed!

The name of Shambho was devised to set fire to you. It was devised to awaken you in such a way that you can never sleep again in your life, to awaken you in such a way that even death cannot put you to sleep.

For me, Shambho is not just a word. It is all that I know. It is all that flows through me. It is the last thing I will utter before I shed my body. It is the password to my very existence.

As a yogi of the upper Velliangiris, my only aim in this lifetime is to allow the torrential grace of these mountains to flow through the valleys and foothills, so it can flood the planet. This cascade of blinding clarity is capable of sweeping through an entire world and transforming it. It is capable of filling every human heart, infusing every creature on this planet.

All it takes from our end is willingness. For willingness is all it takes to allow this abundance to envelop us, to become instruments of this grace, to receive this dimension called Shambho. My entire life work is to bring this willingness into the hearts and minds of humanity.

PART TWO
CHRONICLES

SADHGURU

THE ARRIVAL

What unfolds here are the chronicles not of Shi-va, the ultimate emptiness, or Shiva in his innumerable other mythic forms, but of Adiyogi, the first yogi.

He was not of this planet. He came from another realm called Kailasa.

Why did he come?

Perhaps he saw a planet full of confused people who did not know how to use their intelligence. It is possible he decided to step in and open them up to the ultimate possibility they embodied.

Or, maybe, the earth was the first place he encountered on his travels.

Or, maybe, he was called. Maybe he heard the inner cry of human beings and decided to answer their longing.

With a being of such immensity and capability, all we are left with is conjecture. When one's capability is of cosmic dimensions, every realm is inadequate. He may not have come with a mission. But he was a being with a vision. He had to share it.

He adopted a human form. Lore tells us that when he stood beside a horse, his face was on level with its ears. The southern Indian tradition says that he was twice as tall as an average woman. Based on these accounts, it would seem that he was nearly nine feet tall. The only animals he was seen to ride were an elephant and a bull; he was obviously too big to ride any other creature.

He mastered the human form, and assumed it in different ways. Most of the time, he took on an ideal form and was an extremely beautiful man – nine feet tall, perfectly formed. This image of Sundaresha, the exquisite one, endures in Indian calendar art even today.

Why nine feet? Maybe he got the proportions a little wrong. Or, maybe, knowing the human attachment and identity with form, he realized that his size would enhance his impact as a teacher.

This is why lore describes Adiyogi as *swayambhu* – self-created. He has no parentage, no pedigree, no caste, no community. He is not available to the forces of destiny. He is not available to the forces of karma. He is not available to the normal processes of life. His life is self-made.

Fundamentally, the basis of yoga is just this: to initiate a process of self-creation where the nature of your body, your emotion, your mind, your energy is consciously created by you. This is what Adiyogi did. He crafted his life in its entirety.

He did not come alone. With him were his friends, known as the Ganas. Lore depicts them as misshapen beings. They did not bother with adopting human forms. Or, perhaps, they could not master the human form as he did. They created their own bodies, but their forms stayed amorphous. They lived with him through all his years on earth. It did not matter what form they assumed; they were always the closest to him.

You could think of it like this. If you spilled mercury on the ground, it would turn into lots of individual shapes and blobs. It is so dense that it should be solid, but it is actually a liquid. If you simply bring those separate blobs together, they effortlessly merge and become one again. This is all we are: just little pieces of the planet manifesting as so many different forms and believing that we are independent. The Ganas were like those little bits of mercury. They were unconcerned with taking on fully individualized forms. They were mere extensions of Adiyogi and were content to be just that.

He chose to live in the upper Himalayas. A mountain that came to be known as Kailash was his abode. It was named after the place of his origin. This mountain became the repository of his immense and incredible knowing.

Most of the time, his eyes stayed closed. When he was in ecstasy, he danced. When he went beyond ecstasy, he grew still.

He is often presented in popular imagery as blue in colour. Subsequent divine entities of the subcontinent, such as Rama and Krishna, are also presented this way. This is not without reason. If a realized being leads a life of great stillness, his aura will generally be radiant white. But if a realized being chooses to be active in the world, his aura will be blue. Why? This is because clarity, as we know, is colourless or transparent. When a human being arrives at clarity, the aura becomes transparent. Hence the white aura or halo – an idea with which many are familiar. But this transparence also means one is unable to be active in the world. The moment you take to dynamic action, therefore, the aura turns blue, as blue is the next best thing to transparence. (As we know, a clear sky is always blue.) And so, when he emerged from his meditation and danced, Adiyogi's aura was an electric blue.

Popular imagery also depicts him as covered with ash. When all dross is incinerated, all that remains is ash. This is the stuff of which he was made. It is said ash oozed out of his very pores. This was to indicate that he had burnt every shred of ignorance within himself and was in constant touch with the inner truth.

A legend tells of a yogi who was proud of the severity of his penance. On a certain day, when he was cutting grass in the forest to make a thatched roof for his hut, he accidentally chopped off his own finger. He suddenly saw, to his amazement, that sap was oozing out of his severed finger. He was proud to see that his penance had yielded such a tremendous miracle. He was now convinced that he had attained the ultimate. His vanity came to the fore, and he started believing there was nothing more to be achieved.

Adiyogi decided it was time he realized that his spiritual journey was far from complete. Assuming the form of a mendicant, he accosted the yogi.

'You believe you have achieved the supreme goal,' said Adiyogi, 'But this is not it.'

'What do you mean?' said the yogi. 'Can you not see? I have turned so pure that sap flows out of me. Look at my finger!'

Adiyogi laughed. 'That is nothing to be proud of. Animals eat leaves and roots and make flesh and blood out of them. So, that which was plant becomes an animal, and that which was sap becomes blood. Ultimately, however, plant, animal and man – all of them just turn to ash.'

He asked the yogi to watch as he sliced off his own finger. As he did so, ash oozed out of his wound. Now the yogi became aware that ash actually oozed out of every pore of Adiyogi's body. Awestruck, he realized that a truly enlightened being lives life and death simultaneously, at every single moment. Only he who is constantly aware of the mortal nature of his existence, who knows that the flesh and blood that he carries is nothing more than a heap of ash, is truly self-realized. In incinerating all falsehood within is the making of a yogi. This is the ultimate truth that Adiyogi embodied.

Lore also says that Adiyogi wore a coiled snake around his neck and a crescent moon on his head. The snake is symbolic of an incredible level of perception. Gifted with exceptionally heightened perceptual powers, the serpent represents an advanced stage of existential development. In the esoteric traditions of all cultures, wherever people have delved into extrasensory perception, the snake plays a pivotal role. It is the protagonist of several creation myths, even if some have vilified it, fearing its capabilities.

Since yogis constantly aspire to enhance their perception, the snake's significance in the yogic tradition is not surprising. The only creature on this planet that sees the *akashic* or etheric dimension in the daytime is said to be the cobra. The distinctive pattern of movement and stillness of which it is capable makes it a metaphor for *kundalini shakti* – the vital energy coiled at the base of the human spine – which yoga consciously harnesses for spiritual development. Adiyogi's snake is a symbol, therefore, of his tremendous mastery over the inner life.

The third-day crescent moon upon his head represents his connection with the intuitive and mystical dimensions of life. It also represents intoxication. Lore says that Adiyogi imbibed *somarasa*, the nectar of moonbeams, and was perennially inebriated. At the same time, he was a yogi, a perfect ascetic – a reminder that yoga as a spiritual path has never been opposed to pleasure.

Adiyogi's yogic mastery allowed him the pleasure of being internally drunk and completely aware, fully stoned and fully conscious, at every moment of his life. This, he reminds us, is possible for each one of us. We can generate our own peace and joy internally, without any external stimulus. The path of yoga makes us the masters of our own chemistry, the authors of our own bliss. Once we find access to our own inner intoxication without losing our stability, our lives become an exuberant expression of our joy, rather than a pursuit of happiness.

Intoxicated and alert; dynamic and still; superbly formed and yet in tune with lunar mysteries where things lose all shape and definition; larger-than-life and yet covered with the ash of death – Adiyogi embodied many contradictions all at once.

When he came to the profoundest state of inner stillness, however, he was impervious to the many things happening around him in the world. He was capable of remaining that way until the end of time.

FROM ASCETICISM TO EROTICISM

Those were dark days on the planet. Several tyrannical despots had usurped control from the wiser lawmakers. They imposed their own capricious law upon the land. The benevolent kings, who were in the minority, were powerless against these forces of corruption, particularly those of Taraka, a monarch of overweening ambition and power.

The only one who could restore balance and harmony to such a fractured planet was Adiyogi, the formidable hermit in the Himalayas. But Adiyogi was a recluse and an ascetic. He could not be induced to fight.

Still, the benevolent kings could see that Adiyogi possessed powers that nobody else did. If there was anyone whose intervention could rescue a world spinning hopelessly towards self-destruction, it was he. But no one had the courage to approach him because he was like a flame of overpowering intensity.

Was there any way to squeeze these mysterious powers out of him?

They decided to consult the more easily approachable divine entity, Vishnu.

Vishnu said, 'I cannot approach Adiyogi either. His yogic powers are so immense that I have no idea what is happening within him. If he parts with his incredible knowing, it will only be of his own volition. No one can steal these powers from him. At present, he is unapproachable. First, we need to win his attention, soften him, find a way to make him heed us.'

The question was how. They thought up innumerable plans and strategies. None of them seemed workable. Adiyogi was far too forbidding a figure to be enticed by minor inducements.

Finally, they decided their only hope was a child born of Adiyogi's seed. His offspring alone could vanquish the forces of corruption and restore sanity to a troubled planet.

But this meant Adiyogi had to consent to become a family man. The ascetic had to turn householder.

They approached him as a collective, full of trepidation. Roused from his meditation, Adiyogi was annoyed. 'Why do you disturb me?' he asked.

They laid out their woes before him. 'You close your eyes in bliss all the time,' they lamented. 'You are oblivious to the strife that surrounds you. You have no clue that people around you are in unspeakable states of misery. Should you not be more sensitive to their plight? Should you not do something?'

'What would you have me do?' asked Adiyogi.

That was the question for which they had been waiting. Now, Sati, the beautiful daughter of Daksha, the patriarch of the Vedic sacrifice, was brought before him. 'She is Goddess Shakti herself,' said the kings. 'She has taken birth only to become your partner. You can remain in your ecstasy, if you choose. But if you take her as a wife, your progeny will be able to tackle the problems of the world.'

Adiyogi relented. He walked out of his ascetic life and married Sati.

Now, Adiyogi was the ultimate embodiment of consciousness – a condition beyond the cyclical nature of human compulsion. He was self-made, which means not a shred of compulsion remained in him on the level of the body, mind or emotion. He lived in a state of complete freedom with the ability to respond to the needs of each moment afresh, moving into a new dimension every second. This was not a genteel or civilized man. This was a being in a state of absolute oneness with life – flawlessly non-repetitive, utterly without pretention, ceaselessly spontaneous and inventive. He was life itself.

And so, he simply did what needed to be done in any given situation. Once he married Sati, he gave himself totally to his marriage. He did not see the erotic and the ascetic impulses as conflicting. For him, asceticism was simply a graduation from the limited nature of eroticism. For the sake of the world, he married Sati. But once he did, he surrendered totally to the union.

Immense passion happened between them. The years rolled by. Their lovemaking was recorded as the most intense in human history.

Now that Adiyogi seemed much in love with his bride, the kings were pleased. It looked like everything was going according to plan.

But then the inevitable obstacle reared its head.

One day Sati's father, Daksha, decided to conduct a huge *yajna* or sacrifice. This was part of the great Vedic tradition of the times where oblations were offered at a sacred fire to the accompaniment of hymns and mantras, presided over by priests. It was believed to bring health, prosperity and well-being to the land. As the son of Brahma and a king in his own right, Daksha was determined to make his sacrifice a grand occasion.

Everybody who counted was invited to this sacrifice. All the kings, all the noblemen, all the VIPs were on the guest list. It was going to be a magnificent affair.

But the one person Daksha did not include in his invitation list was his son-in-law. He had always disapproved of his daughter's choice of husband. This strange ash-covered ascetic with his snakes and garland of skulls who lived on the fringes of society made him uncomfortable. Adiyogi had neither caste nor pedigree. Those from the lowest echelons of the caste hierarchy were his companions. His closest friends were the Ganas, utter social misfits. He was often surrounded by wild animals. His favourite lair was rumoured to be the cremation ground. Daksha had no intention of inviting such a being to an event intended for the upper crust of Vedic society.

One day, Sati, who was going about her daily chores, noticed that everybody seemed headed in a certain direction. She stopped the sage Narada and asked, 'Everybody seems to be going somewhere, all dressed up. What is going on?'

Narada said, 'Do you not know? Your father is performing the greatest of ritual sacrifices. Everybody is invited.'

This struck Sati hard because she knew Adiyogi had not received an invitation. She rushed home and poured out the news to her husband. Enraged at this slight, she was determined to attend the function and confront her father.

Adiyogi tried to dissuade her. But when he saw that she was adamant, he sent Nandi, his chief Gana, and some of his other people along with her. He refused to accompany her.

This event dramatizes a prevailing social tension – the conflict between the Vedic Aryans and the earlier indigenous tradition of the subcontinent. Adiyogi represented an older archetype, venerated by the local inhabitants. With the advent of the Aryan settlers, the older cosmology was being supplanted by the newer divinities of the Vedic pantheon.

Sati was furious. Uninvited, she marched into Daksha's sacrifice and confronted her father. 'You have not invited your own son-in-law, the great Adiyogi, the Mahadeva, to your sacrifice. Do you not know he is the greatest of all divine beings? How could you exclude him?'

Daksha's response was abusive. He heaped expletive upon expletive upon his son-in-law. When the sacrificial offerings were apportioned among all the guests according to their stature, there was no offering for Adiyogi. This was the last straw. Sati could no longer bear the disgrace heaped upon the man she loved.

Incensed, she rose. In the middle of the full assembly, she hurled herself into the sacrificial fire and was burnt alive. Since then, in the history of the subcontinent, whenever a woman chose to immolate herself, she has been called a Sati. (In more recent times, the act assumed uglier and more exploitative manifestations, and laws have had to be enacted to put an end to it.)

When Nandi witnessed Sati's act of self-immolation, he rushed back to Adiyogi. He narrated the entire story to him.

Adiyogi heard the news in silence. He sat in stillness for a length of time. A searing rage built up within him – rage against all those who had built a social structure based on entitlement, elitism and exclusion, a culture without compassion, superiority without substance, hierarchy without humanity. As his fury mounted and turned into an explosive fire, he rose, pulled out one of his locks of matted hair and hurled it against the mountain. Out of that lock, an enormous warrior emerged.

Adiyogi's command was clear. 'Go. Let no one, no one who participated in this terrible deed, who condoned it with their bigotry, who upheld it with their prejudice, who endorsed it with their silence, be spared.'

And so, Veerabhadra, the immense warrior, marched into the sacrifice in full fury and unleashed a terrible carnage. He slaughtered everyone, hurled them into the fire, beheaded and impaled Daksha, and turned the site of the great sacrifice into a charred cremation ground. It was a scene of unspeakable devastation.

How do we understand this story?

If human beings seek merely physical and psychological fulfilment, they can live a full-fledged life, as long as twenty-one of the 114 chakras (or energy centres in the human system) are functional. But as a yogi, Adiyogi's attachment to the body was minimal. Physical and psychological needs were trivial for him. The goal of yogic practice is to light up all the 114 chakras. This transforms one into Chakreshwara, Lord of the Chakras. This can render a human being into proportions that are cosmic, enabling one to transform the inanimate into the animate, empowering one to create and manifest new lives and forms.

This is what Adiyogi did. He used all the vital energy in his system to hit the peak of consciousness. Although lore always presents him as a linga, which was interpreted as an erect phallus, it also tells us that he never spilled his seed (except for sacrificial purposes). This means he was capable of marshalling all his generative and creative resources for the highest possibility. The result of this formidable capacity to transmute pranic energy into life was Veerabhadra, a living embodiment of Adiyogi's incredible alchemy. That a single strand of Adiyogi's hair is enough to eradicate an enormous injustice also testifies to his extraordinary mystic capabilities. When the attachment to the body is minimal, fear is non-existent; so Veerabhadra is seen as an embodiment of limitless valour.

When Veerabhadra's desecration was complete, Adiyogi himself came to the scene. He gathered Sati's seared body in his arms. His anguish at what human ignorance could wreak on a beautiful being was so intense that he wouldn't put the body down. Agonized, he began walking. The body began to rot, but he wouldn't cremate it.

He just walked on and on like a bull elephant in a daze of pain, of loss, of helpless fury, across the land.

As he walked, Sati's lifeless body began to decay and fall apart. Various part of her corpse fell across the vast landscape of the Indian subcontinent. Fifty-four pieces fell, according to legend, in different regions. Each dismembered part consecrated the land upon which it fell. Each of these sites, sanctified by his fire and her purity, grew into a centre of immense feminine energy. In this process Adiyogi transformed his loss into a fiery possibility by installing the Divine Feminine across the land. Even today, powerful goddess temples are to be found in each of these locations, known as *shakti sthalas*.

Gradually, Adiyogi returned to his senses. He brought Daksha back to life. Legend says he replaced Daksha's severed human head with the head of a ram. The sacrifice was completed and peace restored. This time, an offering was made to Adiyogi as well, suggesting that the Vedic tradition was now more open to integrating the earlier spiritual heritage into its fold.

Since the Vedic system could not obliterate Adiyogi, it included him. The king of gods for the Vedic ritualists was Indra, but it was clear even to them that Adiyogi far outshone the existing notions of divinity in terms of complexity and sophistication. Adiyogi was too large to be the ruler of the heavens. He was a yogi – a multidimensional phenomenon that they could not understand but could not ignore either. If Indra was king of gods, they turned Adiyogi into Mahadeva, the god of gods, the greatest of all divine beings.

The notion of the divine trinity also belonged to the earlier tradition. In the pre-Vedic tradition, three faces of Shiva were seen as embodying creation, preservation and destruction. They were called Rudra, Hara and Sadashiva. In yogic terms, these three faces correspond to the three main channels in the subtle human physiognomy: *ida* (the left channel associated with the feminine dimension), *pingala* (the right channel associated with the masculine) and *sushumna* (the central channel). So, the feminine, the masculine and that which is beyond both were regarded as three fundamental aspects of Shiva. They were also seen as the three dimensions within every human being.

The Vedic Aryan system later incorporated the same idea, but assigned different figures to the functions of creation and preservation. And so, the well-known trinity – Brahma the Creator, Vishnu the Preserver and Shiva the Destroyer – came into existence.

Adiyogi is traditionally presented as carrying a trident – a mystical emblem of an important number in creation. From the proton, neutron and electron that make up the atom to many other levels of manifestation, the number three is significant. This later found reflection in other spiritual cultures of the world.

The invader's god invariably replaces that of the invaded. But here is a unique case in which the dominant group ended up assimilating the world view of the local population. Although an earlier culture was submerged on many levels, Adiyogi survived erasure and emerged triumphant.

Daksha now made an offering to him in an attempt to appease him, but Adiyogi was not interested. Lore tells us he sent his dogs to consume the offering. He returned to his abode in Kailash, and resumed his ascetic life. He closed his eyes, and became meditative once again.

He did not open his eyes again for a prolonged period of time. New mountains grew around him.

THE POWER OF ONE

It happened...

The evil monarchs of the universe used their occult powers and created three flying worlds. These were called Tripura, the three cities. With these flying cities as their vehicles, the monarchs were invincible. They attacked, raped, plundered, pillaged and destroyed. Gods and human beings were at their mercy. Nobody could stop them because their cities were mobile.

The benevolent forces knew they had to be stopped, but nobody had the power to do so. Then Brahma said, 'Only if these cities are shot down by a single strike can these evil ones be vanquished. Otherwise, it is impossible to kill them as they regenerate themselves.'

But where could they find an archer who could shoot down three flying cities with a single shaft?

They thought long and hard. At last, Vishnu said, 'There is one. Only one.'

Everybody knew whom he meant. Adiyogi was also known as Sharva, the Cosmic Archer.

They went to him, troubled and imploring. 'These three orbiting cities must first come into alignment,' replied Adiyogi. 'Then I shall act.'

So, they now waited for the time when the three flying cities arranged themselves in a single line – a rare occurrence that happened for just a moment once in many cycles of time.

In the meantime, they began to prepare planet Earth as Shiva's chariot. The sun and the moon were its wheels. Brahma became the charioteer. They used Mount Meru, the great Himalayan mountain, as the bow. The cosmic serpent became the string. But there was no shaft. So Vishnu converted himself into a powerful weapon for the purpose.

Fully equipped, they waited. The time drew near. At last the three aerial cities converged in a single line. Looking at all the frivolous preparations that the kings had made, Adiyogi laughed. He simply opened his third eye and shot a single shaft.

The searing shaft pierced the three cities. They erupted into a blazing fireball that tumbled and fell to the Earth in a great white cloud of ash. The evil monarchs, and their terrible rule of violence and injustice, came to an end. A hush fell upon the entire universe.

The good kings and divine beings celebrated, rejoicing at the death of their foes. But Adiyogi merely sat, tears pouring down his face.

They asked perplexed, 'Why do you grieve? You have just vanquished Tripura and the most terrible and corrupt rulers in the universe.'

Adiyogi said, 'It doesn't matter how corrupt they were. They were still a part of me. If this existence is my creation, so is maya – delusion. And the magnificent cities that they built were a product of their ingenuity. I cannot celebrate their destruction.'

He took the ashes that remained of the three cities and smeared them across his forehead in three horizontal lines. He declared, 'Someday, like these three cities, I will destroy the three dimensions of this cosmos.'

And so, Adiyogi came to be called Tripurantaka, the Supreme Destroyer of the Three Worlds.

The 'three cities' continue to wreak havoc in human life. They seem deceptively lifelike, but are essentially unreal for they are not rooted on this planet. They are products of the human mind – ephemeral psychological realms. They are not the consequence of Prakriti, nature, but of maya, the human mind lost in its own hypnosis. The result is an *endless cycle of pride, rage and avarice. Try as one might to destroy them, these flying realms are elusive; they take wing and escape from our grasp.*

When human beings become meditative, it is not that all their negative emotions vanish at once. They cannot. For love and hatred, fear and compassion, joy and misery, agony and ecstasy – all these are the outcome of the same fundamental energy we call life. It is the same energy arranging itself in a million kaleidoscopic shapes and forms. They cannot be vanquished separately because they have no autonomous existence. They can only be dismantled when the fundamental delusion of separateness is destroyed.

As you walk the path of yoga, pride, fury and greed gradually align themselves in a single direction. Pride arises out of a mistaken sense of significance of the self. When this self-importance is threatened, fury is the result, while greed is the fuel that fosters that self-importance. The three are, therefore, inseparable. Once these scattered energies are aligned, the guru shoots them down with a single arrow. The aspirant is then free of a life of psychological oscillation and fracture.

And so, the three lines of ash on Shiva's forehead are a symbolic statement that human fear, rage and lust can be felled. Once they are routed, they can never stand again. When a seeker draws these lines on his forehead even today, this is what he is telling the world: 'I have conquered these three aspects of life. Now I am free to become unbounded.' And thus, the story reiterates an ancient esoteric truth: that the number three is essentially one.

The number three has many other levels of significance. The word trikalagnani has been used in the tradition to describe one who knows the past, present and future. The past, present and future are not three different places; they are a single happening, here and now. When you live this moment profoundly, you experience time not serially but simultaneously – not as three, but one. You then wake up to the fact that mystics have known since the dawn of time: that this moment is eternity.

It is significant that Adiyogi does not hate those whom he destroys. He sees that they are ensnared in their own hypnotic delusion. He knows that when their self-created psychological world is destroyed, the three will perish. And the cosmos will return once more to the immaculate, non-fragmented reality that it always was and will forever fundamentally remain – the domain of Shiva.

SOUND, THE SOURCE

Himavan, the king of the Himalayas, had a lovely daughter named Parvati. She was the reincarnation of Sati. It was her destiny to become the wife of Adiyogi once again. She had nurtured that dream ever since her childhood.

For years on end, Parvati served Adiyogi as he sat in deep meditation, hoping he would recognize their past bond. But he was unwilling to open his eyes and look at her.

In the meantime, the good kings of the world were getting anxious. But they did not know how to awaken Adiyogi. Whatever the provocation, he simply sat, eyes closed, utterly oblivious to everything around him.

They decided to send Kamadeva, the very embodiment of passion, the greatest lover in existence, to arouse him. They told Kama, 'You go shoot your arrow. Once passion arises in him, we will present him with the right woman. Let the offspring come and the world will be taken care of.'

Kamadeva was afraid to approach the forbidding ascetic. But the kings goaded him on. So Kamadeva hid behind a tree, and shot his flowered arrow.

Something pierced Shiva's profound meditation. He opened his eyes. When he saw Kamadeva's attempt to ignite desire in him, he opened his third eye. Kama, the embodiment of desire, was just annihilated.

Adiyogi's third eye is a potent symbol for ultimate spiritual perception. Two eyes can see only the duality of life; they cannot see the beyond. But when one begins to perceive that which lies beyond the physical world, the third eye is metaphorically said to have opened. As a yogi who had transcended the limitations of the physical, Adiyogi's perception simply cut right through the limited world of binaries into which Kama sought to lure him.

Kamadeva's wife, Rati, was grief-stricken. She fell at Adiyogi's feet and pleaded, 'Do something to restore my husband. It was not his intention to disturb you. He was merely doing the bidding of the kings.'

Adiyogi relented. He assured her that in his next life Kamadeva would be touched by a certain incarnation of Vishnu and would then be restored to her as her husband.

Then Adiyogi sat down again and resumed his meditation. Parvati's hopes were dashed.

She had been performing various penances to become his wife. Now, her austerities grew severe. Initially, she sat and meditated. When that did not bear fruit, she became an ascetic. She dropped her clothes. She just used two leaves to cover herself. At this time, she acquired the name 'Dwiparna', the one who wears two leaves.

She continued her asceticism. When this did not bear fruit, she dropped one of the leaves. She was now known as 'Ekaparna', one who wears a single leaf.

To further her intensity, she dropped that leaf too and sat absolutely naked. In the severity of her efforts, she sat for what seemed like an eternity. She was now known as 'Aparna' – one who has nothing to cover herself with and indeed nothing to cover. And her austerities grew more and more severe.

Then, her mother, Mena, unable to bear this, exclaimed, 'U-ma.' This literally means, 'Oh, enough!' (That is how Parvati acquired her other well-known name, Uma.) 'My daughter,' said Mena, 'why do you perform such penance for a man who is a mere beggar, ash-smeared, barely clothed, adorned with skulls, a man without a kingdom, wealth, power, position? A man who frequents cremation grounds. Why would you do this for such a hideous, repugnant being? Stop it!'

But Parvati stayed completely determined and focused. Her intention never wavered.

After many years rolled by, impressed by her ferocious asceticism, Adiyogi opened his eyes. He saw Parvati and her father, Himavan, before him. He blessed Himavan, but he turned away from Parvati. He told Himavan, 'It is improper for you to bring a young woman where there is an ascetic. Take her away.'

Immediately, Parvati said, 'Why do you reject me? And who are you to reject me? You may be Purusha, the fundamental principle in creation. But I am Prakriti, creation herself. Without Prakriti, without nature, there is no action in you. You are just inert. You are incapable of doing anything without Prakriti.'

Adiyogi said, 'I can dismiss and dissolve Prakriti right now. I created her. If I want, I can dissolve her this very moment. There can be no debate on this. Just leave!'

Parvati said, 'If you have the power to dissolve Prakriti, why this asceticism? Why are you sitting in these mountains? These mountains are Prakriti. The air that you breathe is Prakriti. The sky is Prakriti. All that surrounds you is Prakriti. If you dissolve all this, you have no role to play.'

Adiyogi liked her spirit, but he still pretended to be very angry. He commanded her to leave him alone. She refused.

At last, he relented. Impressed by her fortitude and courage, he consented to marry her.

Even today, iconography and poster art present images of Goddess Kali standing on the chest of an inert Shiva. It is a powerful image. It is Kali or the Goddess who can consign Shiva to inertness or infuse him with dynamism. This is not a war between the sexes. The Kali image is instead a visual metaphor of the interdependence of the two dimensions, a reminder that the masculine is lifeless unless invigorated by the feminine.

That is what Shiva's drum or *damaru* indicates. The damaru is a symbol of the meeting of two triangles. These are the masculine and feminine dimensions that Adiyogi mixes up. He makes both intermingle, because without these two, life will be devoid of beauty and meaning. If the feminine is not recognized and honoured, existence becomes one-dimensional. Adiyogi's damaru is an echoing reminder down the centuries that these two dimensions are not oppositional. They are complementary.

But although Adiyogi married Parvati, he remained a living anomaly: a dispassionate ascetic who happened to have a partner. Something had changed this time. The all-consuming ardour that characterized his earlier union was absent. Parvati was his consort, the woman he loved, but even more fundamentally, his disciple.

The marriage of Adiyogi and Parvati was a grand affair. Parvati was the only daughter of Himavan and Mena and they were determined to give her a fine wedding.

On the appointed day, all the guests arrived in their finest attire. Everyone was invited because it was Adiyogi's wedding. The somebodies and the nobodies, the upper castes and the outcasts, the good kings and the bad, the divine and the depraved – all of them attended. Since Adiyogi was seen as Pashupati, the Lord of Nature, all the birds and beasts came as well. And, of course, the snakes wouldn't miss it, so they came too. The insects weren't excluded either. It was a huge celebration. Human beings, gods, goblins, demented beings, ghosts, animals, worms, insects – everyone was on the roster. This was an event very unlike Daksha's sacrifice, which was open only to the A-listers of Vedic society. Here, every living creature was present.

Finally, Adiyogi arrived with his retinue of Ganas. Smeared from head to toe in ash, his hair matted and wild, his eyeballs rolled up, he staggered in, utterly intoxicated. With him was his entourage of unruly companions, all chattering in an incomprehensible tongue. Their speech sounded wild and cacophonous.

Mena saw this, horrified. 'What? Am I supposed to hand over my lovely, fragile daughter to this barbarian, this brute of a man?' And she fainted.

Then some guests went to Adiyogi and told him, 'The bride's mother has lost consciousness. She cannot bear your form.'

Adiyogi shrugged. 'This is how I am.'

But then Parvati came to him and pleaded. 'My mother is in a state of shock. She doesn't really know who you are. Please assume another more pleasant aspect. Show her, for my sake, your magnificent form.'

Adiyogi gave in to please her. He transformed himself into Sundaramurti, an embodiment of resplendent masculinity, the handsomest man on the planet. He stood there, splendid and shining, and quieted his raucous Ganas. When Mena regained consciousness, she looked at him and said, 'I only wish my daughter could marry someone like this!'

Another interesting incident occurred at the time of this great wedding.

When the marriage ceremony was on in full swing, the priests turned to Adiyogi. When the bride is about to be given to the groom, it is customary to ask about the groom's background, his parentage, his family tree, the time and date of his birth, his astrological details. So they asked, 'Please tell us your antecedents.'

Adiyogi just looked down and stayed silent.

A great hush fell upon the proceedings.

Then the sage Narada picked up his stringed instrument, the *ektara*, and began to play a single note.

The priests kept repeating the question. There was no reply.

The priests were in a hurry, because the time was auspicious, and they did not want to delay the wedding. But Adiyogi continued to sit quietly, while Narada continued to play his note.

Finally, they asked, 'What is going on? Why is he sitting quietly?'

Narada replied, 'Because he is swayambhu, self-created. He has no parentage.'

Adiyogi had no past – literally and otherwise. And in the yogic tradition, this is the ultimate aspiration that he represents – freedom from the repetitive cycles of nature and culture. He reminds us that it is possible for every human being to aspire to this freedom. If we distance ourselves from our attachments and identifications, it is possible for all of us to be self-created.

On the traditional path of asceticism or *brahmacharya* in the subcontinent, the seeker still performs the last rites for his parents. This symbolic act denotes a conscious distancing of the self from genetic and cultural memory. Cyclical nature means going round in circles – in other words, not getting anywhere! The aim of the spiritual process is to break through these compulsive cycles, whether physical or psychological, to reach the condition of authentic freedom.

'And why are you plucking the string?' the priests asked Narada.

'The entire creation is rooted in a reverberation, a sound. Out of his mastery over all sound and all creation, he has created himself. I am plucking this string because reverberations of sound are Adiyogi's parentage. Nothing else.'

HIMALAYAN HUMILITY

It happened…

The cosmic grapevine was buzzing with talk about the raas leela,
*the night-long ecstatic parties that happened around Krishna on full-
moon nights.*

*These were nights of utter intoxication, where everyone was drunk
on the moon,* soma, *and the dazzling presence of Krishna. These
celebrations, suffused with song, dance, moonlight and madness, became
the talk of the universe. People began travelling long distances just to be
there on this magical night.*

*News reached even Adiyogi on the remote snow-clad summit of
Mount Kailash. He decided to join the revellers.*

*He came down the mountains into the plains of the subcontinent. He
reached the banks of the river Yamuna. On seeing a boatman, he hailed
him and asked to be ferried across to Vrindavan.*

'Where are you going?' asked the boatman.

*'Well, everyone is talking about the raas leela on the other side. I
want to join the party.'*

*'But you cannot go like this,' protested the boatman. 'No men are
allowed. At the raas leela, Krishna is the only man. Everyone else must
be a woman.'*

*Adiyogi was taken aback. 'What! Me? A woman? How can I go
as a woman?'*

The boatman said, 'It's no use. If you go as a man, you will never know the real taste of raas leela. If you want to go, you have to go as a woman.'

Then Adiyogi got into the spirit of things. He said, 'Can you get me a costume?'

So the boatman went home and brought him his wife's sari. Adiyogi, the epitome of masculinity, dressed himself in the worn, frayed sari of the boatman's wife, and went to the raas leela. And there, no doubt, he danced and revelled in Krishna's presence like none other. For in the dance of euphoric dissolution, there was none to match him.

Devotion essentially means receptivity, a trait associated with the feminine dimension. You could be a man, but if you do not know the feminine within you, you will never experience authentic devotion. The nature of the masculine dimension – or pingala, in the yogic terminology – is assertion, conquest; the nature of the feminine – or ida – is receptivity, devotion. Every human being embodies both these dimensions.

As one who was absolutely at ease with both aspects within himself, Shiva had no qualms whatsoever about shrugging off one role and adopting another when required. Although he is seen as the ultimate embodiment of masculinity, he remained unshackled to any gender identity. Uninhibited, he slipped effortlessly between roles and definitions, which accounts for the bewilderingly diverse manifestations he assumes in sacred myth.

MYSTIC PROGENY

Adiyogi consented to marry Parvati, but this time it was a marriage with a difference.

He did not approach marriage with the same single-minded fervour he had brought to his relationship with Sati. He played the role of a husband when needed, but spent most of his life as an ascetic.

Tradition says that he disappeared for long periods of time. Did he return to Kailasa? Perhaps.

There are a number of Sanskrit verses or *shlokas* that refer to Adiyogi as Yakshaswaroopa, one who has the form of a Yaksha. Yakshas, according to lore, were beings who came from a celestial realm. They were known to be beautiful and ageless. Adiyogi fits this description perfectly, because there are no records of his birth, his childhood, his old age, or his death. The people around him were always described as other-worldly beings with distorted forms and boneless limbs, who spoke an unintelligible language. These were the Ganas who probably returned with him periodically to Kailasa.

His long spells of absence left Parvati forlorn and desolate. The story goes that once Adiyogi disappeared for over eleven years. A lonely Parvati decided to take matters into her own hands. She applied some sandal-paste all over her body, mixed the unguent with some earth, and crafted the form of a human child. With her tantric powers, she breathed life into this child. And thus a boy was born. Parvati had the son she had longed for, a child moulded from her very body.

Several years later, Adiyogi returned with his Ganas. Unaware of his return, Parvati went for a bath. She instructed her son to stand guard while she bathed. When Adiyogi strode in to see his wife, he was stopped by a boy he did not recognize. The boy took pleasure in displaying the authority invested in him by his mother. He resolutely denied Adiyogi entry.

Adiyogi looked upon this strange boy, whom he perceived as not even real, and with a flick of his sword, lopped off his head. And so, this boy who was an incomplete being – a manifestation of Parvati's longing, but without the contribution of the masculine dimension – lay there, headless.

When Parvati discovered what had happened, she was anguished. 'What have you done?' she berated her husband. 'How could you? Return my son to me!'

In an attempt to appease her, Adiyogi severed the head of one of his willing Ganas and replaced the boy's head with a new one. Thus the boy acquired the name Ganapati, Lord of the Ganas. He now became a combined embodiment of the Earth and the beyond, the terrestrial and the transcendent, and a complete being for the first time.

Symbolically, the boy was incomplete because he was the offspring of Prakriti without the induction role played by Purusha. He was the child of Shakti – creative, exuberant and vital – but without the dispassionate, transcendent wisdom represented by Shiva. Once his head was replaced, he came alive as a new being – an unmatched and auspicious blend of material and metaphysical wisdom.

The story of the transposed head is to be found in myths across the world. Each time it re-enacts a primal truth: that limited self-understanding must be decapitated for a more profound and inclusive wisdom to take its place.

Somewhere along the way, a misunderstanding has arisen in popular Indian culture which holds that an elephant head was used as a replacement for the missing head. But this is obviously a later interpolation. Since the head of a Gana was used – amorphous in shape with an extension that was a boneless limb – popular culture probably turned it into an elephant head over time. It is significant that the boy was called Ganapati, which literally means Lord of the Ganas, rather than Gajapati, Lord of the Elephants. He now represented the union of the transcendent knowledge of the Gana with the natural auspiciousness and abundance of the Goddess.

The boy grew into one of the wisest and most knowledgeable of all Ganas, and is venerated to this very day as one of the subcontinent's favourite and best-known gods, Ganesha or Ganapati, the supreme vanquisher of obstacles, an embodiment of an incredible intelligence well beyond human potential, the guardian of all gateways, patron of all portals, worldly and mystical.

In the meantime, the tyrannical monarch, Taraka, was growing increasingly troublesome. As mute spectators to his arrogance, the good kings of the world grew more anxious than ever.

They approached Adiyogi again. 'You must do something,' they pleaded with him. 'We had urged you to marry so you could bear a child and put an end to these problems.' What they hadn't bargained for was the fact that no woman could bear Adiyogi's child, because Adiyogi was not, in fact, of this planet.

However, in his compassion, Adiyogi now decided to intercede more decisively in human life. He allowed his seed to fall to the Earth. This incredibly potent seed was swallowed by Agni, the fire element. Whatever is offered to the fire element acquires an effulgence that reaches every other dimension around it. And so, six women in high states of purity and receptivity, who happened to be warming themselves at the fire, suddenly found themselves pregnant.

However, so scorching was this seed that they could not bear its terrible heat in their bodies. In just three and a half months, they expelled these foetuses, unable to bear their intensity. When Parvati saw these foetuses were Adiyogi's progeny who embodied six sterling qualities, she thought, 'If only all these qualities were to be found in one single being, how wonderful it would be!' She used her mystical powers to merge these six foetuses into one, and nurtured the child in a lotus leaf.

Through this unusual process of amalgamation and incubation, an exceptional child was born. It is because he was six beings merged into one that Kartikeya was known as 'six-faced' or 'Shanmukha'. This was a unique mystical experiment wherein six individuals were fused into a single body, which produced a child of phenomenal strength and capability.

Kartikeya grew rapidly into a glorious young man and set forth on his mission. He annihilated Taraka, the evil despot, and fulfilled the purpose for which he had been conceived.

Kartikeya's entire life represented a crusade against injustice. A well-loved legend tells the tale of his earliest experience of injustice that shaped and catalysed his later life's mission.

It happened…

On a certain day, Adiyogi was relaxing with his family and pets on the foothills of Kailash, basking in the warmth of the sun in the lower altitudes of the Himalayan slopes.

With him were his two sons – Ganapati, the offspring who now
sported the head of a Gana, and Kartikeya, the beautiful younger
son whose radiant presence embodied the intensity of six beings.
Shiva's favourite bull, Nandi, Ganapati's playmate, the mouse,
and Kartikeya's pet, the exquisite peacock, were also part of this
relaxed family party.

A devotee of southern India now appeared, bearing a basket
of mangoes as a gift for Adiyogi. These were mangoes of mouth-
watering sweetness and lusciousness to be found only in the fertile
soil south of the Vindhya Mountains. During the long journey
north, however, most of the mangoes had turned rotten. Only one
unspoiled fruit remained. This ripe mango was placed as an offering
at the feet of Adiyogi.

As any father would, Adiyogi handed over the fruit to Parvati,
and said, 'Give it to the children.'

The moment they saw this delectable golden fruit – a rarity,
utterly inconceivable in the icy fastness of the upper Himalayas –
the two sons were enchanted. In one voice, each claimed it as his
own.

But unlike the apple or pear, the mango was a fruit that could
not be divided into two equal halves. How were they to apportion
it between them?

Playfully, Parvati proposed a contest to resolve the impasse. 'Let
there be a race,' she said. 'Whoever circumambulates Mount Kailash
and returns first shall win the fruit.'

No sooner were her words uttered than Kartikeya set off like a
bolt with his pet peacock.

But Ganapati, the weightier of the two, was in no hurry.
Unperturbed, he simply ambled up to Adiyogi and Parvati, circled
them three times, and extended his hand for the mango.

Adiyogi was amused. 'You did not participate in the race,' he said.
'What makes you think you should get the mango?'

The wise Ganapati, whose transposed head was replete with celestial sagacity, replied, 'All human experience springs from within. The external world is entirely an inner happening. The race was to circle Mount Kailash. But you, my parents, are my Kailash. You are my world, you are my universe. So, must I circle an illusory perception rooted in maya? Or must I be true to my inner experience? I have circled my Kailash not once but three times, and my brother is nowhere in sight. So the mango is rightfully mine!'

And so it was.

Then Kartikeya arrived, flushed and jubilant, and was elated when he saw that his brother had not even begun the race. As he drew closer, however, he noticed the telltale smear of mango and the supremely contented expression on his brother's face. The passionate, quick-tempered youth, who embodied the intensity of six lives in one form, flew into a rage at this perceived injustice.

He walked out in a blaze of anger, vowing to avenge every injustice, right every wrong, redress every grievance he ever encountered in the world. Leaving behind the idyllic family fold at the foothills of Kailash, he headed into the prosperous, culturally complex lands of the southern peninsula where material resources were abundant but distributed unequally.

In the course of his journey, he annihilated many whom he perceived as perpetrators and agents of inequity and wrongdoing. This bloody journey brought him to the farthest reaches of the south.

After a short militant life devoted to waging war against all the unjust forces on the planet, he began to awaken to the futility of violence. When you are in a state of rage, whatever seems logically incorrect appears inconsistent and unfair. And so, he went about slaughtering everything that did not fit into his ideas of right and wrong. Then he found that at this rate, he would have to destroy every human being!

Chastened, he withdrew and decided to shun violence. He washed his bloody sword clean for the last time in the flowing River Dhara in southern India, and climbed up a mountain. A temple stands to this day to mark the place where he meditated before he began his ascent. He finally left his body on the peak of the mountain. This is Kumara Parvat, literally the Son's Mountain (named after Adiyogi's fiery son), a well-known pilgrimage site in the state of Karnataka.

Even today, if one goes up this hill, it is evident that something incredible happened there. The place radiates an overwhelming energy. It is clear that a yogi of the highest attainment relinquished his physical form here.

Symbolically, Kartikeya represents the masculine and martial dimensions of the divine. He is Purusha actualized. He is the result when Adiyogi, the hermit, turns warrior, when the mendicant turns into a man of action. Unlike Ganapati, he was created by Adiyogi without the contribution of Parvati. He was the product of Purusha, but not of Prakriti. Significantly, he does not turn into a yogi until he discovers the more receptive, or feminine energy, within him. It is when he finds compassion that he truly embraces the dual nature of his inheritance as the child of Prakriti and Purusha, Shakti and Shiva, ida and pingala.

Many years ago, when I visited this incredible site with a small group, we camped outdoors. I found it difficult to sit or lie down anywhere on this hill. At night, when I entered my four-foot-tall trekking tent, my body kept assuming an upright posture, dismantling the entire tent.

It became clear to me then that Kartikeya, as an advanced adept, had left his body in a standing position. Normally, when yogis leave their body, they are cross-legged; on some occasions, the body is relinquished in a supine posture. But Kartikeya is unique in that he left his body standing, symbolic of his uncompromising stand against injustice.

This young yogi attained liberation thousands of years ago, but signs of his radiant presence endure. To this very day, many pebbles on this unique mountain are six-faced. And peacocks are still to be found in abundance, trailing their resplendent plumage across the many verdant forests and rugged slopes that he traversed in his lifetime.

THE SIDEKICKS OF SHIVA

The tales of Shiva's devotees in popular culture are legion. Many of these devotees have been revered as great yogis in their own right.

Devotion is not a dissection of life; it is a total embrace. There is no shred of sanity involved, and no way to recover from it. It is the deepest form of intelligence. For devotion means you have voluntarily dissolved all resistance within you so that the divine can transpire as effortlessly as your breath. When the divine becomes a living force within you every moment of your life, it is an experience of indescribable ecstasy. Devotees may look crazy to others, but they are often having the best time on the planet!

Here are two well-known stories from southern India. They remind us that devotees do not aspire for power; that is their power. They do not seek to become special; they seek instead to become ordinary – extra-ordinary, in fact. For anyone on a spiritual journey, this is the goal.

It happened…

Sage Poosalar was steeped in poverty, but determined to build a magnificent temple for his beloved Shiva. Every day he diligently went about building this temple, brick by brick, entirely within himself. This inner exercise took him years.

The king of the land was also planning to inaugurate a big Shiva temple that he had commissioned. The night before the grand opening,

Shiva appeared in the king's dream. 'I cannot attend your temple inauguration tomorrow,' he said, 'because Poosalar has invited me too. I cannot deny Poosalar: he is my truest devotee. There is no temple that can match his.'

The king was nonplussed. He wondered who could have built a temple grander than his own. He set out in search of Poosalar and finally found him in a dilapidated hut in the poorest district in town.

'Why does Shiva intend to attend your inauguration and not mine?' asked the indignant king. 'Show me your temple.'

'The only temple I have,' replied Poosalar, 'is in my heart.'

This well-known legend reminds us of a profound truth: if devotion overflows, divinity will follow and serve you. It has no other choice.

One of the reasons the word 'spirituality' arouses such suspicion in our world today is the fact that it is pursued by several who have little or no control over their imagination. Unfortunately, these unbridled flights of fancy have given rise to the view that the spiritual process is intended only for those who can boast of past-life experiences or visions of angels and celestial lights. But imagination is strictly a faculty of the mind. It has nothing to do with the existential.

Looking at the lives of a few devotees of such calibre, others have tried to use the imagination to emulate them. But it will not work because Poosalar's inner temple was not built of the imagination alone; it was built of flawless, unwavering, single-minded devotion. His consciousness was so crystallized that the distinction between what is real and what is not real had been obliterated.

If such a person envisions a certain form, that form just comes alive for him. This is not imagination. This is creation. If you can invest your very life energies into the process of imagination, it will become creation. As for Poosalar, he was united with the very source of creation; he had become one with the Creator.

It happened...

Allama Mahaprabhu was a great sage and Shiva devotee in the southern state of Karnataka in the twelfth century. He was spiritual guide to a remarkable fellowship of mystics in this vibrant time in spiritual history. A subtle and profound being, he authored thousands of couplets of exceptional depth and mystical insight.

One day, another great mystic and Shiva devotee named Goraksha encountered Allama. Goraksha was a yogi on the path of kayakalpa. 'Kaya' literally means body; 'kalpa' means rejuvenation. This is the ancient yogic science of creating not just health, vitality and longevity, but taking the body to another dimension of strength and competence altogether. Goraksha's yogic virtuosity had made his body as hard and stable as a rock.

There are certain yogic practices that entail purifying and mastering the five elements in the human system. With advanced practice, one can attain bhuta siddhi – complete mastery over the elements. Such practitioners can live well beyond the normal span of human life. This accounts for innumerable stories in the yogic lore of adepts who have lived for extraordinary lengths of time.

At this time, Goraksha was already believed to be about 280 years old. He challenged Allama: 'You are considered a great yogi and Shiva devotee. Let us see what you are capable of.'

Goraksha pulled out a diamond-tipped sword, handed it to Allama and said, 'Take this sword and strike me hard on my head. See what happens.'

Allama was amused. With both hands and with all his might, he smashed the sword down on Goraksha's head. Goraksha stood there like a rock, utterly invulnerable. The sword just bounced off his head.

Then Goraksha said, 'Now that you have used this sword against me, I am also permitted to use it against you.'

Allama agreed. Goraksha picked up the sword and slashed fiercely at Allama. To his amazement, the sword passed right through

Allama's body. Allama continued to stand there, unaffected. If Goraksha's yoga had made his body like a rock, Allama's yoga had made his like thin air.

Goraksha continued to swish his sword this way and that, but it passed through Allama time and again. Then Goraksha had the humility to bow down and concede defeat. 'I know the yoga of strength,' said the yogi. 'But I do not know the yoga of dissolution.'

And so, he became Allama's disciple.

This apocryphal story is yet another reminder that for a devotee, vulnerability is not weakness. As a devotee of Shi-va – literally 'that which is not', or 'no-thing' – Allama had dissolved into the object of his devotion. His readiness to embrace that limitless no-thingness had made him invincible. His willingness to become vulnerable had made him, in fact, invulnerable. This is the tremendous power that accompanies a chosen powerlessness.

The distinctive hallmark of the spiritual culture that Adiyogi bequeathed to the world is that it does not seek to create worshippers, but yogis. Yogis do not aspire to worship god. Instead, they seek to embody the sacred themselves. They do not seek to adore the divine. They aspire instead to dissolve, to become one with divinity. The yogic culture is not god-oriented – and this is what makes it an invaluable contribution to a world ravaged by wildly conflicting definitions of the divine.

Adiyogi's legacy offers you the licence to believe in the god of your choice, or not to believe at all. And if you do not find a god to your taste, it allows you the freedom to create one. That is how the Indian subcontinent arrived at an exuberant 330 million gods and goddesses at last count! To see the divine in a tree, rock or elephant is not considered absurd because every speck of creation is seen as a portal to the ultimate reality.

These gods were not mere imaginary toys. Instead, this culture evolved a science of consecration, an entire technology of god-making. These deities are referred to as yantras – literally, machines to enhance life in *all its manifestations. And so, the deity becomes a stepping stone to your liberation. How you reach your liberation, whether with or without a yantra, is entirely up to you. But your destination is always mukti or freedom – which ultimately means freedom from all doctrines and beliefs, and from all man-made gods as well.*

Devotees are sometimes disconcerted when I speak of the divine as a tool or device. But this is the audacious insight of this tradition: it dares to see devotion as a technology and even god as a device!

Does that mean it denies the sacred? No. It invites you, instead, to experience the ultimate, rather than draw conclusions about it. To experience the ultimate you have to be willing to obliterate the self-created boundaries of individuality, you have to be willing to dissolve. That state of unbounded freedom is a state of oneness with Shiva – an unconditioned state beyond physical experience, beyond imaginative speculation, beyond all conceptual understanding.

ULTIMATE INCLUSION

Thus far, we have followed the well-known life story of Shiva. Versions of this story are known to people all across the Indian subcontinent.

Like all world myths, this tale of passion and grief, rage and valour takes us on a journey to the darkest recesses of our consciousness. It reminds us of all that it means to be human. Nothing is too ugly, nothing unacceptable. Everything is part of the great, complex, magnificent dance of life.

But Shiva is also the protagonist of a yogic story. It is a story that reminds us of a far more primary identity: that of Dakshinamurti, the original teacher and first spiritual master. It is here that the essence of Adiyogi's legacy lies.

Adiyogi's first disciple was his wife. When Parvati saw the ecstatic state in which her husband seemed to be all the time, her curiosity was piqued and a deep desire was kindled.

One day she could contain herself no longer. 'I want to have what you have,' she insisted. 'Show me how to get there. I am willing to do whatever it takes. Teach me.'

Adiyogi saw Parvati was in earnest. He also saw her desperation to have children was her way of seeking fulfilment. His compassion now came to the fore.

He told her gently, 'This is not the way to find fulfilment. Whether you have one child or a thousand, you are still not going to find the answer. Do not waste your life like this. Do not be led by the instincts of your sex and biology – that only offers a limited possibility. There is another way to fulfilment.'

And thus opened up what are known as the *Shiva Sutras*, the science of yoga expounded in its absolute beauty and splendour.

There are various ways of delivering this science. Depending on different dimensions of perception and receptivity, the method of transmission varies. If an aspirant is in a certain state of resistance, it is delivered one way. But if the aspirant is in a deep state of openness with you, it can be delivered in quite another way. Because there was a deep intimacy between Adiyogi and Parvati, he chose absolute inclusion as the way.

This intimacy need not be understood as sexuality. Intimacy essentially means an absence of resistance. When the other person is absolutely receptive, you do not have to use a sledgehammer to break through any wall.

The ultimate idea of intimacy in Eastern culture has been the *guru–shishya* or master–disciple relationship, because this is a relationship in which two beings meet. Two bodies meeting is the result of mere compulsion; it is not considered to be real intimacy. It is not considered wrong, but it is not profound either.

Since the body is gathered from the food we eat, the physical is regarded as something external to us. The yogic system calls it the 'food body' or *annamayakosha*. In many temples of the East, there is a flagrant display of worldly life in all its manifestations. Physical intimacy in all its variations is displayed all over temple walls. But this is only external. The intimacy of the sanctum is of a different kind altogether. The temple walls acknowledge the physical world, but the sanctum is an invitation to go beyond.

So, Adiyogi told Parvati, 'Give up this effort to procreate in all kinds of desperate ways. Come, sit on my lap. Let me show you the way to your ultimate fulfilment.'

Now, this might just look like a man's trick to have a woman on his lap. But no, Adiyogi was not just willing to have his beloved on his lap; he was willing to make her a part of himself. When Parvati demurred, he invited her again gently, 'Come, Devi, sit on my lap.'

When she was seated on his lap, he proceeded to address her in the most loving and tender ways you could address another human being. In every *sutra* or aphorism, he called her the 'resplendent one', the 'beautiful one', the 'tender one', the 'sweet one'. This was not an attempt at seduction; this was to develop an intimacy so she was absolutely free of any residual resistance.

And as the intimacy deepened, one of the most celebrated conversations in the history of the spiritual quest unfolded. For Parvati had innumerable questions for him about truth, the meaning of life, the nature of reality from the seed to the universe, the dimension beyond the changing cycles of birth and death, space and time. Her many impassioned, searching questions and her free articulation of doubt remind us that debate is not incompatible with the spiritual process. Adiyogi's bequest to the world was a spiritual process that was not founded on commandment but dialogue, not on certainty but discovery. As this conversation deepened, he brought Parvati closer and closer to a point where she became a part of him.

Most people have only enough love within them to fulfil domestic requirements. If, however, love has to transcend arrangements of social, economic and reproductive needs, and become a possibility of ultimate union, something else is needed. If you have to make somebody a part of you, you must be willing to rip out a part of yourself.

And this is what Adiyogi did. He tore out a part of himself and made his consort a part of him forever. Hence the iconic depiction of Adiyogi as Ardhanareeshwara – half-man and half-woman.

It is interesting that though Adiyogi is held as the ultimate symbol of masculinity, he is half a woman. He is a reminder that no man is complete without acknowledging the feminine aspect of himself. It is also a reminder that the masculine and feminine are present in equal proportions within an individual. If the masculine and feminine attempt to fuse externally, it never lasts – and all the troubles that come with it are a familiar ongoing drama! But if the two meet within, the individual is transported to an abiding state of ecstasy.

The crescent moon on Adiyogi's head is a reminder that one half of his brain is lunar. The moon has been regarded as feminine because of the influence of the moon on the cycles of the female body. But every human being – whether man or woman – has a brain that is partly solar and partly lunar. It is just that the lunar has a subtler manifestation in the masculine and is more apparent in the feminine; the solar is more apparent in the masculine and a subtler presence in the feminine.

When Parvati and Adiyogi acknowledged the other within themselves – the feminine and the masculine, Shakti and Shiva, the lunar and the solar – they turned ecstatic. The union testifies to the fact that existence was birthed in absolute ecstasy – *ananda*, a joy that is within the reach of all who seek it with passion and single-mindedness.

Once she became one with him, Adiyogi expounded the path of self-realization to Parvati in a multitude of beautiful and intimate ways. This came to be known as *tantra*.

Tantra essentially means 'technology'. It is not an independent system, like yoga, which is an internalized, highly sophisticated path. In the present context, tantra and yoga are often viewed as separate but, in reality, tantra is just one aspect of yoga.

Historically, when some people found the yogic path too internal and challenging, they were given a few external tools – ways of using the food they ate, the water they drank, for instance – towards their inner development. That was regarded as an independent process and, in time, came to be called tantra. But essentially, tantra is the technology of employing external means for spiritual growth. When you use materiality – either your own body or the planet – to raise your consciousness to a certain pitch, it is tantra yoga.

So, with Parvati, Adiyogi expounded the path of self-realization in many ways. Since the sutras are offered in a state of intimacy, they are subtle, persuasive and gentle.

On the one hand, the human body is just a perishable mass of flesh, driven by simple instincts. On the other hand, if maintained in a particular way, it can turn into an invitation to the divine. It can become a gateway to the ultimate. And so, Adiyogi touched Parvati in 114 different ways, activating her body as an instrument. He opened up for her the knowledge of the self as the source of creation, not as a creature. If you open up the self as a creature, all you see are anatomical parts. This is biology. If you open this body up as creation, however, you witness the entire cosmos. This is yoga.

As he started his transmission, Parvati took on various forms. These are the many faces of the Goddess. She became pleasant, she became unpleasant. She became love, she became fear, she became grief, she became longing, she became compassion, she became fury...

She took on every kind of form that could be evoked within the human consciousness. As she took on these forms – from the subtle to the increasingly intense – the seasons changed, the atmosphere in the world changed because, she was, after all, Shakti, the fundamental energy behind existence. So as she went into the many phases of her consciousness, everything around her transformed.

Then, Adiyogi brought her to a state of equipoise where she realized that all this was just a play of energy. To harness that play of energy and channel it to its ultimate end is the science of yoga.

She realized that she was none of these, that she was beyond all these forms and faces. She understood that the human body was a doorway to the beyond, that the physical organism was a mirror of the universal organism, that creation was in fact a key to the cosmos.

One did not have to be amputated for the other to be achieved. The gross and the subtle, the dense and the divine, the corporeal and the cosmic, were part of the same continuum. Shakti was inseparable from Shiva. However hard they convinced themselves of their autonomy, they were one. And their fundamental nature was joy. Everything else was and has always been just a small ripple – finite, minor, transient – in the limitless truth of ananda.

What transpired between Adiyogi and Parvati was not a teaching. It was a transmission, a sharing. It was possible because Adiyogi made Parvati a part of himself. The complexity of life and life-making material can never be understood within the narrow limitations of logic. And so, Adiyogi, as a guru, adopted a method so subtle that a logical or analytical mind will wonder, 'Could such an approach really work?' But it worked miraculously for Parvati and she became fully enlightened.

After that, Parvati and Adiyogi went into a state of unbridled ecstasy. They wandered the Himalayas in uncontrollable rapture, oblivious to the changes of the world around them. The seasons changed. The years rolled by. Their passion showed no signs of abating. Their ecstasy showed no signs of diminishing. Their union was complete.

UNITY OF THE SEXES

Ardhanareeshwara is a unique mystical symbol. A delightful legend illustrates the difficulty encountered even by a great sage in grasping all its implications.

It happened...

Bhringi was a wise sage and ardent devotee of Adiyogi. Every morning, Bhringi came and circumambulated Adiyogi as a mark of respect.

One morning, Parvati happened to be sitting beside her husband. But Bhringi, single-minded in his devotion to Adiyogi, walked between them and circled only his master. He wanted his pradakshina or ritual circumambulation to be only for his guru.

Adiyogi was amused. Parvati was not amused. She cast a look at her husband who said, 'Move closer. He will circle you too.'

Parvati moved closer. Bhringi saw that there was not enough space for him to circle only Adiyogi, so he transformed himself into a mouse. He was now able to circle just Adiyogi. Parvati was excluded once again.

Adiyogi's amusement grew. But by now Parvati was intensely annoyed. So, to placate his beloved, Adiyogi lifted her and placed her upon his lap.

Bhringi was not to be outwitted. He changed into a tiny bird and flew around Adiyogi alone, excluding Parvati once again.

Now, Parvati was fuming. So, Adiyogi just pulled her close and made her a part of himself. Now the left half of his form became hers and the other half remained as it was. He turned into Ardhanaareeshwara – a composite androgynous form of male and female.

But Bhringi refused to admit defeat. When he saw this, he turned into a bee and circled Adiyogi's right leg.

His childlike fervour was amusing. But Shiva did not want him to get lost in his devotion and miss the ultimate nature of existence. So, Adiyogi assumed the yogic posture of siddhasana, which does not allow any space between the right and left leg. Now, there was no way for Bhringi to circumambulate the right leg alone. If he wanted to perform the ritual pradakshina, he had to honour both the masculine and feminine principles.

The sage now finally came to his senses and realized how myopic his devotion had grown. His literalism gave way to a more inclusive understanding. He realized that both the masculine and feminine spring from a singular source. He bowed down to both dimensions, a chastened man.

The fundamentalist impulse can creep up on a devotee in many ways. Devotion is the quickest path to the divine, but it also has its pitfalls. The tendency to turn literal, or dogmatic, or to believe that one's path or one's notion of the divine is superior to all others is a seductive challenge.

This is why it is said 'that which is not' must never be named. To name is to limit, to curtail. At the same time, Shiva is given innumerable names. This may seem paradoxical, but there is a deep intelligence that underlies this.

The sum total of all these names is a representation of the universe in all its magnificent complexity. It is a representation of the unfathomable mysteries of existence. These can never be fully captured in any doctrine, or image, or concept, or shrine, or creed, or symbol. The welter of contrary names for the divine is testimony to the fact that Shiva can only be experienced, never understood. The yogic path reminds us of this truth again and again.

AND NOW, YOGA

Once Parvati gained more control over her energies, she grew still. Gradually, after a certain phase of stillness, she began to hear the clamour of the world. She looked around her, and the suffering in the world was so stark compared to the ecstasy within her that compassion poured out of her. She was blissful, but she had no means to transmit it.

So she sought Adiyogi.

She said, 'What we have between us is wonderful. Don't you think every human being deserves a taste of it? Shouldn't such an experience be shared?'

Adiyogi laughed and said, 'Do not take that step. And you will never make me take that step. It is futile. People are ignorant by choice, not compulsion. No teaching is needed. No method is needed. If they are willing, my grace is always available. What stops them from receiving it? Until now nobody has made an attempt. Why offer grace where it is unsought? Why concern yourself with those who are not thirsty?'

But Parvati would not leave him. In every possible way she tried to convince him that he must play a more active role in hastening the evolution of consciousness in the world.

Adiyogi said, 'You do not know the intricacies of this science. You are only enjoying the fruit of it. You do not know the trouble I will bring upon myself in trying to teach it to the world.'

He knew the struggle and the pain of talking about something which is not in people's experience. He knew it would only be misunderstood. It was a thankless job.

He said, 'I do not need this complication. You have what you desired. You just remain ecstatic. That is enough.'

When he kept refusing, Parvati hired a consultant. She went to Vishnu in his celestial abode and she said, 'I know it is your desire to know what Shiva is experiencing, and to make this happen to everybody. I am trying to get him to share this, but he refuses. How do we get him to impart this to others?'

Vishnu said, 'See, when he sits there as a yogi we are totally powerless. There is nothing we can do; he is way beyond us. But when he is with you as a man, there are things that you, as a wife, can do, if you are willing.'

And he whispered into her ear.

She returned, armed.

And when they were together as man and woman, she said, 'I am sorry I ever troubled you with all these requests. I can clearly see that you are not capable of transmitting this to others.'

Adiyogi said, 'What? Me? Not capable?'

She said, 'No, no, it doesn't matter. I know you cannot do it.'

He fell for it.

And that is how the very first yoga programme took place on the banks of an incredibly beautiful Himalayan lake called Kanti Sarovar, almost fourteen thousand feet above sea level.

The participants were seven committed spiritual aspirants who had remained in Adiyogi's presence for many decades. He had always ignored them.

As they watched him alternate between ecstatic movement and utter stillness, it was obvious to people that this man had something that nobody else had. They wanted to know what it was. But when he remained motionless in meditation for years on end, most of the curious bystanders disappeared. Only seven remained. They could not tear themselves away from his side.

When they expressed their desire to learn from him, Adiyogi dismissed them. 'This is not entertainment. This takes something else. You do not have the mettle for it.'

When they persevered, he gave them a few preparatory steps and said, 'Do this for a time, and we will see.'

Days rolled into weeks, weeks into months, months into years. But his attention never fell upon them again. They continued to perform a variety of austerities to become deserving candidates.

It was their commitment that made the difference. Thousands of people came to him with the same thirst, but only seven persevered.

After years, on the first full moon night after the summer solstice, Adiyogi's eyes fell upon them. He could not believe these seven had become such wonderful shining receptacles. He could not ignore them any longer.

For the next twenty-eight days, he observed them closely. He saw they had reached remarkable levels of purification and readiness.

On the next full moon day, he could not withhold himself any more; he faced south and spontaneously turned teacher. On that first full moon after the summer solstice – a day which is still observed as Guru Poornima – Adiyogi became Adi Guru, the first guru on the planet. Because he turned south to teach – symbolic of the southward journey of the sun after the summer solstice, a period known as *Dakshinayana* – he is also called Dakshinamurti, the great teacher who faced south.

In time, these seven disciples would become the celebrated seven sages, the Saptarishis. They carried Adiyogi's knowing to different parts of the planet and became crucial players in the unfolding of events in the world. Wherever they went, those places became the crucibles of world civilization.

What did Adiyogi expound to these seven disciples?

He imparted the most comprehensive system of human self-exploration imaginable. 'Between you and enlightenment,' he told them, 'there is an infinite distance.' With Parvati, Adiyogi had employed the path of intimacy. But with the seven sages, he brought forth the most severe and rigorous ways. With Parvati, he demonstrated that there was no distance between an individual and enlightenment. With the seven sages, he spoke of an 'infinite distance', but he also demonstrated that true intimacy is not different from infinity. For ultimately, there is no difference, he explained, between zero and infinity, the present moment and eternity, the here and the hereafter. The aim is to reach the point where there is no boundary line between the human being and existence, between individual and infinity. That is true intimacy and that is also enlightenment.

He taught them in seven different formats, based on the seven fundamental dimensions in the human system. This historic exposition happened through the solar cycle of twelve and a quarter years.

He left out nothing. He was so complete, so complex, so consummate a teacher that he offered a dazzling variety of methods. These were not philosophies or teachings. This was a profound existential science. Not all of the instruction was verbal. Much of it was through direct transmission.

The basis of Adiyogi's wisdom was that every particle in existence

– including the sun, moon and planets – has a consciousness of its own, but every atom does not have a discerning mind. Once consciousness arises with a discerning mind, it is a powerful possibility. This is what makes human life unique and capable of enlightenment.

However, human discernment has gone off the rails. This is why individuals experience themselves as isolated in this world. This is why they live in delusion and ignorance. Enlightenment is meaningful only because human beings are invested in ignorance. A plant, on the other hand, does not need enlightenment. It is simply life itself.

Light is important only because people experience the terror of darkness. If there was no darkness, light would have no meaning. More specifically, if one could see in the dark, light would have no meaning!

Human discernment does not mean, therefore, simply dissecting or dividing existence. That is a mental game, a psychological circus that can keep human beings engaged for a lifetime. The same capacity for discernment can be employed for a deeper purpose. True discernment is the capacity to distinguish between the bound and the boundless, between the psychological and the existential, between delusion and truth, between maya and life. This is when human discernment becomes a powerful and unique possibility.

Every creature has its qualities, but a human being has no fixed qualities, explained Adiyogi. This is why people constantly surprise us. They are capable of being utterly base and startlingly sublime – crass and bestial one moment and radiantly divine the next. Since there is no established quality, there is no human being; there is only human *becoming*. Human beings can become whatever they want. Nature has given them this freedom. This means that from the moment of creation, human beings cannot evolve unconsciously. If they want to evolve, they have to evolve *consciously*.

'What then stands between us and our ultimate nature, our freedom?' asked the sages.

Adiyogi's reply was succinct: yourselves.

He drew their attention to that aspect of the human mind called manas. This comprises memory – vast silos of memory, he asserted. In other words, what keeps us from our freedom, he implied, is our programming. This conditioning goes deep. It operates on unfathomably complex levels that are seldom apparent to us. It is these layers of memory that separate us from our authentic nature.

Our lives are ruled by eight forms of memory, Adiyogi explained. These are elemental, atomic, evolutionary, genetic, karmic, sensory, inarticulate and articulate.

The five elements that make up the human body stamp their own imprints upon us. Similarly, the dance of the atoms is distinctive in each individual because of past memory. Our evolutionary journey shapes our biology, while the genetic codes or software within us determines our individuality. Karmic memory – a vast storehouse of impressions honed by our past actions – plays a further role in moulding qualities and propensities. The daily maelstrom of sensory stimuli also leaves a residual impact, determining the ways in which our bodies and minds react to our world: this is sensory memory. Additionally, there is the sediment of the unconscious – or what Adiyogi called inarticulate memory. Finally, there is the impact of all the conscious information we carry – which he termed articulate memory.

All these levels of memory, said Adiyogi, individuate us. They are responsible for who we are today. They make us unique. They gift us with distinctive capabilities and desires, habits and idiosyncrasies. They are responsible for the diversity of human life. But the same memories imprison us. They shackle us to self-definitions we cannot rid ourselves of. We may celebrate our limitations and turn them into badges of identity. But whether gold-plated or iron-barred, a cage is still a cage.

What human beings term 'knowledge', said Adiyogi, is mere accumulation, pure memory. The volume of memory, however vast, is always limited. Human knowledge is always within bounds. Ignorance, however, is boundless. If our knowledge is wide, it could just mean, therefore, that our prejudice is wide!

If we have an active intelligence, however, we become non-stop, effervescent seekers, never certain but always joyfully confused. And seeking, Adiyogi declared, is not a spiritual idea. If we are not identified with the limitations of our knowledge, seeking is entirely natural. The way he illuminated, therefore, was a movement from indoctrination to intelligence, information to borderless ignorance, accumulation to aliveness.

As the sages absorbed this information, they were filled with new questions. 'But why?' they asked at length, echoing the query that so many have asked since the beginning of time. 'Why did it happen? Why did memory turn oppressive? Why did individuality turn into imprisonment?'

Memory is neither right nor wrong, replied Adiyogi. It is neither good nor bad. It is simply the nature of physical existence. At first, consciousness was a great stream of purposelessness. Then this great stream began to seek purpose. And so, it curved.

That curve of consciousness was the birth of matter. It was the birth of cycles, which are the basis of physical existence. It was the birth of form, of individuality, of diversity, of purpose. But that very purpose turned, over time, into bondage.

When consciousness realizes it is bound, it yearns to be free again. It seeks to unloose itself from the cycles of the physical. It seeks to break out from the convolutions of the psychological. It seeks to return to a state it dimly remembers – a state no longer inscribed by memory, a state free of intent. It seeks to return to what it once was – a boundless, purposeless unity.

'But *why?*' the sages persisted. 'Why must this game from purposelessness to purpose to purposelessness be played out? What is the *point* of it all?'

Adiyogi laughed. Purpose is the need of the mind, he asserted. Existence is not utilitarian. Existence is a phenomenon beyond utility. The mind thinks of utility only because it is a scavenger in perennial hunter-gatherer mode. Human individuality has been gathered. But with enlightenment, there is nothing to gather or to give, nothing to take or to return, nothing to accumulate or to surrender. Life simply *is*, that is all. 'And if you were simply dripping ecstasy, as I am,' he told them, 'you would not even ask this question.'

It is because of identification with the limited cyclical process of physicality that human beings find life burdensome. That is why they ask about the purpose of carrying this burden. That is why they ask about the profit for this labour of life. That is why they ask about the reward. A mind that has been castrated and domesticated, he implied, cannot see the point of a rampaging bull elephant, for it has lost the innate understanding of the wild where life is beautiful and purposeless all at once.

Life has no use at all, declared Adiyogi. It is simply a phenomenon. Little acts have purpose. But life is not framed within the narrow grid of utility. It is beyond frames. It is beyond grids. It is beyond utility. If you have a taste of this existence beyond purpose, of life beyond sense, you are enlightened.

'It is possible for us to speculate and create endless stories about why creation happened,' said the great teacher. 'If I tell you a story, you can either believe it or disbelieve it. Either way, it will get you no closer to the truth. I am not here to tell you a story. I am not here to tell you why. I know the way out of the game, and that is all that counts. Never mind why. Let me show you *how*.'

And that 'how' gradually unfolded into the great science of yoga. So remarkably multidimensional was Adiyogi's exposition that it took even seven brilliant, intensely focused men a very long time to comprehend it.

Adiyogi expounded paths that worked regardless of a person's level of evolution. For every person on the planet, there is a way, he insisted. That was the uniqueness of the system he imparted. No one was left out.

The goal that Adiyogi set before humanity was liberation – liberation from the tyranny of compulsiveness and unconsciousness, liberation from the cycles of the body and the mind. This gave rise to a spiritual legacy that still endures in many subtle ways. The ethos of the Indian subcontinent was crafted to enable all to seek their liberation, irrespective of their context. Every aspect of life – whether you loved or prayed, studied or worked, meditated or sang and danced – was only aimed at your liberation. Everything else was secondary. Your entire life was oriented towards your emancipation. Whatever you did, your life was your pilgrimage.

The human energy system, said Adiyogi, is a microcosm that mirrors the way the entire cosmos is organized. This is a fundamental yogic insight: the geometry of the individual and the universe are identical.

The basis of Adiyogi's wisdom was that everything that we seek to know about existence lies right within us. The way out, he declared time and again, is *in*.

He pointed out that with just a little focus, the yogi can perceive three dimensions in the forehead. Subsequent cults of Shiva have called this the seat of ultimate perception or the third eye, but the science of yoga refers to it as the *agna chakra*. A complete existential map can be found right here. Within the agna chakra are three manifestations in ascending order – Rudra, Hara and Sadashiva – which reveal how existence has unfolded. Creation began with a roar, then moved into a settled state, and finally reached a transcendent state. All these three dimensions – the beginning, middle and end – are manifested in the human physiology.

He explained what yogis down the ages have subsequently realized through inner experience: that there are 114 chakras or energy centres in the body. The basic bio-energy system, which we refer to as 'prana', flows through 72,000 *nadis*, or pathways or channels, and meets at 114 junction points called chakras.

These energy centres are not visible. If one cuts the body open, they will not be seen, said Adiyogi. But as one becomes more and more aware of the movement of energy, one realizes that energy is not moving at random, but in particular patterns. The energy moves through 72,000 patterns or pathways, which meet at 114 points in the body – 112 are within the physical body and two are outside the body.

'How many paths exist to human liberation?' asked the sages.

If one uses the human system, only 112, he replied. The last two chakras, he said, are only accessible to those who have transcended the physical. For everyone else, there are 112 chakras, each of which can be an entry point to the divine.

Lore tells a particularly interesting story about Parvati at this time. When he was expounding the mechanics of life to the seven sages at Kanti Sarovar, she was a silent witness. She was already self-realized. But what was now unfolding before her was a completely different dimension of exploration. It fascinated her that something that had happened to her so effortlessly was now being presented as such a complex process. She knew it experientially, but she did not know the journey intellectually.

There was a difference between her and the sages: she was in love with him; the sages were in love with what he had. Because of her level of perception and receptivity, she did not go through the steps; Adiyogi just took her directly to the peak of attainment.

When he said there were 112 ways in which a human being could attain liberation, she, already being enlightened and, above all, his wife, couldn't resist asking, 'Why only 112? There must be more.'

He was deeply absorbed in exploring the mechanics of life; he was not merely expounding a teaching or philosophy. He saw this whimsical comment as a disturbance, and waved her aside, saying tersely, 'No, no more.'

She said, 'I'll find more.'

He said, 'All right, you go and find more.'

Stung by his dismissal, she went away and tried to explore various ways on her own. After many years of fruitless practice, she returned. Adiyogi was still deeply immersed in his exchange with the Saptarishis.

As his wife, Parvati had the right to come and sit beside him. But she came and sat one step below him. She did not want the sages to know what had happened, but she did want to admit that she had failed at the challenge she had taken upon herself. Sitting a step below him was a symbolic acknowledgement of defeat.

Adiyogi now sought to relieve her of her embarrassment. He turned to her and began explaining the subject at greater length.

The human body, explained Adiyogi, is incapable of further physical evolution. One can learn to use it better. But it cannot evolve further, unless there are some basic changes in the physical laws that govern the solar system.

It is an insight that seems to be confirmed by modern neurology. We are told today that in order to increase the capacity of the human brain, either the number or size of neurons would have to be increased. If more neurons are stacked into the brain, there would be far too much static, which would reduce clarity. If the size were to be increased, the volume of energy required to sustain these neurons would be too great for the human body to generate. Given the manner in which the human body is built, therefore, the capacity of the brain cannot be increased, only used more effectively. This is why the path of yoga seeks not to enhance the capacity of the brain but to access deeper dimensions of intelligence – an intelligence beyond the intellect – that enables one to function in a more effective, organic and integrated way.

Only the first phase of evolution in the cosmos is physical, Adiyogi pointed out. After that, the evolutionary process shifts to other dimensions. So, if rooted in the body, there can be only 112 ways by which a human being can evolve to the ultimate possibility. But if one transcends the human system, there are as many doorways to the beyond as there are atoms in the universe.

While there are 112 chakras in the body, Adiyogi highlighted seven dominant dimensions from the base of the spine to the crown of the head: the mooladhara, the *swadhishthana*, the *manipura*, *anahata*, *vishuddhi*, agna and sahasrara. Any spiritual journey can be seen as a progression from the root chakra, the mooladhara, to the fontanelle, the sahasrara. There are innumerable practices in the yogic sciences that empower a seeker to journey from one dimension to another. This gave rise over time to the seven basic schools of yoga.

Adiyogi's exposition of the seven schools, founded on the seven basic dimensions, was trailblazing and laid the foundations of the entire yogic science. However, for subsequent yogis and masters, it has not been necessary to understand these highly complex algorithms; it has been sufficient to know how to *access* these.

For Adiyogi also offered four simple points of access, offering not merely a science of incredible profundity but a perennially state-of-the-art technology. There are four fundamental levels, he said, on which a human being can be touched and transformed: body, mind, heart and energy.

The distinctive feature of his wisdom was that it did not exclude any aspect of the human being. Not a single aspect of the individual was denied, suppressed, shunned or trivialized because of its inherently transient or perishable nature. No aspect was seen as an obstacle on the path. Instead, yogic science turned all potential hurdles into stepping stones, all impediments into building blocks.

In time, this gave rise to four broad types of yoga: the yoga of action (*karma yoga*), the yoga of intelligence (*gnana yoga*), the yoga of emotion (*bhakti yoga*) and the yoga of energy (*kriya yoga*). Since every human being is a unique cocktail of the same ingredients, these four yogas have to be mixed, said Adiyogi, in differing doses for each seeker. Once these four disparate dimensions are harnessed, integrated and aligned, the human being can turn into a tremendous spiritual possibility.

As the discussion continued to unfold on the banks of that limpid Himalayan lake, the questions deepened, and Adiyogi's responses grew more fine-tuned and subtle.

'What is the primary prerequisite of a seeker?' asked the sages at one point. 'Is it important that they refrain from inflicting harm either in word or deed? Is it important that they be patient, joyful, peaceful, compassionate?'

A seeker, said Adiyogi, must, above all, be unwavering. He was the first to declare that if one stayed long enough with any emotion, liberation was inevitable. 'Even if it is anger, just stay with it – you will get there. If it is love, stay with it – you will get there. The wise will choose pleasant emotions; that is always a more intelligent choice. But it does not matter. As long as you keep unwaveringly in any state, you will reach your destination.'

The problem with human beings, he said, is not the direction, but the lack of focus and fickleness of approach. If you do anything intensely and strongly enough, he insisted, you will, at some point, hit a dead end. And the divine *is* the dead end.

This unconventional insight was one of the significant features of Adiyogi's wisdom – testimony to the fact that it did not grow out of social morality, but out of the highest state of consciousness. It is why one of his many names is Achaleshwara, he who is absolutely unwavering.

One day, as they contemplated the infinite vistas of knowledge unfolding before them, the sages asked their master in wonder, 'How vast is the universe?'

The entire universe can be packed into a mustard seed, he answered briefly.

A mustard seed? They were perplexed.

'But how can we understand this?' they asked. 'The universe seems so vast, so complex, so diverse. How can we ever hope to understand its mysteries? How can we learn its ways? How do we penetrate its secrets?'

By then, Adiyogi was so thoroughly bored, he just made a gesture with his hand. He didn't even bother to speak. He simply indicated the number 'five'. The sages gradually understood what he meant: 'Take charge of the five elements and you will know the universe.'

Adiyogi is important to humanity as the master of yoga – Yogeshwara – and as the gateway to liberation – Mukteshwara. But he is also vital as Bhuteshwara, master of what the yogic system regards as the five basic elements: earth, water, fire, air and *akash* (often translated as ether, essentially the subtlest dimension of physicality). The mastery of yoga and mastery of the five elements go hand in hand. They cannot be separated. Without a fundamental understanding of the elements, the body will remain an unconscious, compulsive process. Without understanding the basis of the body, it can never be transcended. As Bhuteshwara, Adiyogi bequeathed to the world a highly refined science of the elements that laid the foundation for this understanding.

To make a simple lentil soup in the modern-day kitchen takes at least thirteen ingredients. To make the cosmic soup, on the other hand, takes only five! What an utterly brilliant and diverse creation! The human organism is just the product of the mischief of these five in different proportions: 72 per cent water, 12 per cent earth, 6 per cent air, 4 per cent fire, and the rest akash. Though the percentages of the first four elements remain reasonably constant, the percentage of akash can be enhanced. To what dimension one's akashic element is enhanced will determine the possibilities of human perception.

It was this key to the staggering diversity of creation that Adiyogi offered his seven disciples in that simple gesture. Once the five elements are mastered, he implied, you have direct access to the very source of creation. You can now put together and dismantle the human and cosmic system at will. The seven sages and Parvati were astounded at the utter simplicity of that formulation.

'Once you take charge of these elements,' Adiyogi declared, 'you are in charge of your existence. When you have taken the very process of life and death into your hands, you are the supreme architect of your destiny.'

The most basic form of yoga to this day is the cleansing of the five elements, known as *bhuta shuddhi*. This determines several aspects of the individual, from health and longevity to psychological balance, spiritual growth and mystical capability. (In theory, it is termed the cleansing of the five elements. In practice, however, only *four* elements truly need to be worked at, for akash is an element that does not require any purification.)

An advanced practitioner of yoga, however, seeks not merely to cleanse the elements but to master them. This mastery, known as bhuta siddhi, enables the yogi to integrate and dismantle the body at will. Many great yogis, referred to as *nirmanakayas*, have demonstrated this ability down the ages. The yogic tradition is full of accounts of great beings who have been able to dematerialize their bodies at the time of death, leaving behind no sign at all of their material existence. These accounts have, over time, been regarded by the outside world as outlandish rumours or cheap magic tricks. They are neither.

Adiyogi is himself regarded as 'self-created', because he could create his own body the way he wanted. Sometimes he was an exquisite man; sometimes he assumed a distorted form. This was possible because of his absolute control over the elements.

Finally, as he drew to the close of his remarkable exposition on the elements, Adiyogi reminded his disciples of their choices. 'Either you master these five elements,' he said, 'or you simply surrender to the cosmic intelligence, and liberation will be yours.'

His wife had already embraced the other way. Through surrender, she had reached her destination. On the other hand, his seven disciples – men of blazing intellect, curiosity and determination – chose, not surprisingly, to pursue the path of mastery.

The spiritual process anywhere in the world to this very day is of two basic kinds: the path of ecstasy and the path of awareness. These are known in yoga as the path of *samadhi* and the path of *pragna*. Adiyogi's uniqueness lay in the fact that he embodied and imparted both possibilities.

Every spiritual process that has subsequently arisen on the planet has accentuated either awareness or ecstasy. Pragna is a calibrated path of measurable stages to reach the ultimate. Samadhi is a journey without stages, an absolute abandonment of self, a love affair multiplied a zillion times over in terms of intensity and insanity, a leap into a bottomless void. On this journey, there are no milestones, no signposts, no indices by which to measure personal progress. It is not the way of those who seek the slow, graduated fulfilment of the path of the mind. For those who are concerned about the direction and distance they have travelled and the nature of the path, samadhi can represent a terrifying option. However, without at least a tinge of samadhi to infuse a measure of joy into one's life, the path of pragna can often turn dry and laborious.

The paths of contemplation and ecstatic dissolution remain the two main streams that flow through the complex network of spiritual paths in the world to this very day. Individuals tend to gravitate towards either one or the other, based on their temperament and orientation. As the motionless ascetic and the exuberant dancer, Adiyogi epitomized both and offered both possibilities to his disciples.

When all the seven disciples were fully enlightened, Adiyogi proposed to send them out into the world to disseminate the yogic sciences. He was certain that the day would dawn at some point in the future when the entire world would embrace some yogic tools.

At one point the sages asked him, 'Why so many methods? Surely one or two are enough? Why do we need so many?'

The entire world will take to it one day, declared Adiyogi. That is why many methods are needed. Not everybody will be inclined towards the same method. 'People are different in orientation, temperament and ability,' he said. 'As you need different seeds for different soils, as different terrains spawn different life forms, as different forms of life seek different habitats, so shall different human beings seek different methods.'

The sages obviously had their doubts. 'We have no idea who these people are, or if they even exist. We have no clue if there is anyone interested in such a science in the strange lands to which you propose to send us. Will all of them really take to this?'

Your business is to plant the seed, Adiyogi reminded them. Just one seed can turn the entire earth green. Preserve the potency of the seed. When the season is right, the planet will turn green.

As his twelve-year exposition drew to its close, the great yogi offered his disciples a vision they would never forget. He exploded into a state where all the 112 methods of attainment found physical manifestation, offering his disciples access to the deepest innards of creation. It was a vision of the very core of the cosmos in all its profundity and magnificence, a vision of the unfathomable mysteries of the universe. It was the most overwhelming moment the sages and Parvati had ever witnessed.

Awestruck, each of the sages absorbed whatever they could from this sacred and spectacular vision. But Adiyogi raised his hand and stopped them. 'Take these in equal proportion,' he instructed them. So, each of them took sixteen methods for himself. Through this act, Adiyogi divided himself into seven parts and found manifestation in seven different beings to spread his wisdom across the world.

When the sages were realized, empowered by extraordinary knowing and ready to set out on their mission as teachers, Adiyogi asked them for a ritual offering of gratitude, a *guru dakshina*. The seven were nonplussed. As spiritual practitioners, they had no material possessions. What could they possibly give? They stayed silent.

Only diminutive Agastya stepped forward. He now offered to Adiyogi all the sixteen ways that he had received. He was prepared to go out into the world with nothing at all. Having renounced everything, he also became, in many ways, the most complete instrument or medium for Adiyogi.

The other sages followed the example of Agastya. They returned the sixteen ways offered to each of them. It is based on this act that the traditional *guru pooja* – the daily veneration of the guru principle in the East – takes place to this very day with sixteen ritual offerings made to the spiritual master.

As they prepared to leave, the sages asked their guru apprehensively, 'How will we manage when you are no longer with us? How can we access you in times of need?'

So, the master imparted to them a process. This has been preserved to this day in the Kashi Vishwanath temple in the sacred town of Varanasi. It is known as the *Saptarishi Aarti* and is an elaborate process. The priests who perform it now may not be aware of the experiential dimension behind it, but they do know how to keep the process alive.

When I went to Varanasi recently, and witnessed this process one evening, I was amazed because I did not expect the priests to be able to create something like this. In a matter of about one-and-a-half hours, they built stacks and stacks of energy. It was absolutely fantastic. While they probably had no idea of what they were creating, they had at their disposal the technology to create something quite incredible. This is how many methods of yoga have been transmitted. The practitioner is not required to believe in it, or even know how it works. If one simply learns to use it, it is effective.

So, Adiyogi gave this process to the Saptarishis with the assurance: 'Whenever you do this, wherever you are, I am with you.'

The sages were still full of misgivings. 'What if we are not accepted in these strange and remote lands? If people oppose us, or seek to harm us, will you be there for us? Will you come to our aid when we call upon you?'

Adiyogi looked at them incredulously and replied, 'I shall sleep.'

The sages fell silent at this cryptic reply. It was only later that they understood that activity was their business. Adiyogi's stillness was his greatest strength, his most profound grace. That stillness was their anchor and their most valuable ally in the world. It would always be available to them.

Having returned all their hard-earned wisdom, they prepared to leave, empty-handed. But it was their very spirit of renunciation that now bore fruit. Renunciation, or refusing to identify with that which one gathers (however precious it may be), is the ultimate doorway to knowing. In their emptiness, the sages now resembled none other than their master, the primal yogi who had dissolved into the boundless emptiness that underlies all existence. As they set forth into the world, all the 112 ways found complete expression in them.

The sages had believed that tearing themselves away from their master would be the hardest thing they would ever be called upon to do. However, they found, to their amazement, that the distance manifested as oneness, and his absence became an irrefutable and enduring presence in their lives. They were not, and never would be, alone.

In his bid to disseminate his science to the farthest reaches of the planet, Adiyogi dispatched his sages to distant parts of the world.

Agastya was sent south to what proved to be the most spiritually fertile region. Another went to South America; another to North Africa; another to Central Asia; yet another to South East Asia; and another came down to the lower part of the Himalayas (or what is now referred to as the Indian Himalayas). The remnants of the work they did in these regions are evident even to this day. The last sage remained with Adiyogi. The nature of his work is not mentioned anywhere in the tradition. But he remained with his eyes closed almost all his life, working on a very subtle plane.

The sages did different kinds of work in the regions to which they had been assigned. Wherever they went, they left behind traces of a refined understanding of geometry, which manifested in an upsurge in mathematics, astronomy, astrology and other sciences, as well as sophisticated feats of architecture and engineering. It is likely that the sudden spurt in human knowledge and civilization on the planet was due to their intervention. For Adiyogi had entrusted his profound life-altering wisdom in the hands of no ordinary men.

Agastya, who went to the southern part of the subcontinent, is said to have lived a life that was almost superhuman. Legends tell us that he walked across the entire southern peninsula. Even today, the southern states of India bear evidence of his presence: there are temples dedicated to him, there stand the centuries-old progeny of trees that he planted, the caves in which he meditated. They say he lived over 4,000 years. Whether he did, we will never know. Perhaps out of love, his devotees added a zero or two to his age! (Since zero is the outcome of the mathematical genius of India, we retain the right to use it as liberally as we choose!) But if one considers the distances he travelled by foot and the extent of his impact, it is obvious that he lived an unusually long life.

Agastya ensured that every human habitation south of the Vindhya Mountains had a spiritual process – not as a teaching, a philosophy or a religion, but as a way of life. His work is still visible in the culture of southern India. Although recent generations are rapidly losing it, you will find every home still has its simple practices – how to sit, how to eat, how to study, how to receive. He integrated yoga into the culture, so that the benefits are unconsciously reaped even today. Most people may not be aware that they are practising yoga but, in many ways, they are beneficiaries of Agastya's capacity to make this complex science into an everyday affair. For every domestic or social activity, there are traditional postures (*asanas*) and gestures (*mudras*), all of it oriented around one single goal: liberation.

Among the seven sages, Agastya was the ultimate in *kriya yoga*. The very word 'kriya' – a profound system of internal action – is synonymous with him. Since he demonstrated a near-miraculous mastery of the human energy system, practitioners of kriya yoga naturally trace their genealogy to him. This is not to claim a pedigree, but just to express gratitude to a remarkable man who lived as a true embodiment of Adiyogi's wisdom.

THE SCIENCE OF SOUND

A beautiful story tells of a yogi's discovery of the transformative possibilities of a mantra, the science of sound.

When unmanifest existence – often referred to as space or silence – began to reverberate, the first manifestation was sound. The reverberations of sound later consolidated into physical form. The capacity to use sound, the primal reverberation, in a certain way can be transformational. This is the science that underlies the concept of the mantra.

It happened…

One day, an accomplished kriya yogi went to Shiva and complained, 'Do you hear your devotees creating a racket in the world with their deafening chants of "Shiva Shambho"? I am sure you never intended this cultish nonsense. What will these incantations accomplish? Can't you put a stop to these absurd superstitions?'

Kriya yogis are those who aspire to attain mastery over their life energies. As their virtuosity increases, some are filled with disdain for devotees who seem to be on perpetual emotional overdrive.

Shiva listened to him, amused. Then he said, 'Why don't we experiment? There you see a worm crawling by. Go to it and utter the mantra. Let us see what happens.'

The yogi agreed. He went to the worm and said, 'Shiva Shambho.'

The worm promptly fell dead.

The yogi was aghast: 'How did this happen?'

Shiva did not reply. Instead, he pointed to a butterfly and said, 'Look there.'

The yogi looked and found himself entranced by the beauty of the butterfly. Then Shiva said, 'Now utter the mantra.'

The yogi looked in the direction of the butterfly and muttered, 'Shiva Shambho.'

The butterfly fluttered to the ground, dead.

The yogi was now in deep turmoil. He said, 'What is this? If I just utter your name, one creature after the other falls dead. Enough! I don't want to say it any more!'

Shiva ignored this. He turned and looked at a deer that was cavorting around in a nearby glade. He said, 'Do you see that exquisite deer?'

The yogi looked and was drawn by the grace of the animal. Shiva said, 'Why don't you utter the mantra again and see what happens?'

With trepidation, the yogi uttered the words, 'Shiva Shambho.'

The deer crumpled to the earth, a lifeless heap.

The yogi was horrified. 'No! No more can I say this.'

Then somebody brought their newborn child to Shiva for his blessings. Shiva turned to the yogi and said, 'Why don't you utter the mantra in this infant's ears?'

The yogi said, 'No, I refuse to do this! I am already responsible for the deaths of the worm, the butterfly and the deer. I will not utter this terrible mantra ever again.'

At that point, the child sat up and said, 'Please utter the mantra just once more.'

The yogi was speechless and wonderstruck.

'I was a worm,' said the child, 'but when you uttered the mantra, I became a butterfly. You uttered the mantra, so I became a deer. You uttered the mantra, so I became human. Utter the mantra once more, just once more, and I will become divine.'

'JUST DRINK'

Parvati was enlightened. So were the seven sages. Now Adiyogi's cronies, the Ganas, grew restless.

They were his people. Like him, they had created their own bodies. Unlike him, they had not mastered the process of crafting the human anatomy, and had created distorted forms for themselves. But it did not matter what form they had; the Ganas always saw themselves as mere extensions of him. An organism can multiply; a simple amoeba divides itself and becomes many. This is how life happens. This is how the Ganas happened too. The Ganas understood that Adiyogi needed many extensions for his work. They were willing to be just that.

But now, they thought, 'Parvati is having a good time. These seven sages seem to be having a good time. Are we missing out on something? What about us?'

Adiyogi laughed and said, 'Don't bother with this yoga and this *bhoga* – this science and this seduction. That is for those who are enamoured with their own form. Just do the regular thing. You just drink of me, and let us dance. That is enough.'

They looked at him, utterly gleeful that they had no work to do for their ultimate well-being. They simply drank him in with each breath and danced in ecstasy.

The story is a reminder that yoga is not against pleasure. Yogis are not anti-intoxication; they are just greedy and unwilling to settle for small pleasures. They know a glass of wine gets you a little buzzy but leaves you with a headache the next morning! You can enjoy inebriation only if you can be totally drunk but hundred per cent alert.

Recent scientific research reveals that the human system is capable of producing its own narcotic if it is maintained in a certain way. It is a completely self-contained system. And, what's more, this is a narcotic which has a tremendous impact on health, well-being, alertness and perception. This chemical has been termed Anandamide (after the ancient Sanskrit word 'ananda', which refers to the core of life as blissfulness). If a sufficient amount is generated in the system, an individual can be intoxicated and fully awake at the same time. So, what Adiyogi disclosed, in effect, was that there is a whole marijuana mountain inside you! If you cultivate it properly, you could be stoned and yet stable, exuberant and yet aware all the time.

As an autonomous path, however, he offered this only to his Ganas, and not to anybody else. Why? This was because their forms were amorphous and self-created; they did not have the defined limits of the human anatomy. For yoga, the practitioner needs to be embodied and individualized. The Ganas did not have this problem.

The lore tells us they smoked hash and made a cocktail called soma, which they drank plentifully. And then Adiyogi told them, 'Drink of me.' So, they drank *him* in – and that was enough.

It is important to remember that Adiyogi himself did not use substances to get stoned or high. He actually brought himself *down* by partaking of these substances. Even when he was in a physical relationship with Parvati, for him sex was a downward trip.

He said to her, 'What you are experiencing as the highest pleasure, what makes you scream in ecstasy – that is a huge step down for me.'

That is when she said, 'I don't want this any more. I want what you have. I want to know what you know.' And so the legendary tantric transmission began.

Adiyogi used various means to root himself in the body. Lore says he ate wild boar meat, smoked hash, drank soma, just to enable himself to function as a physical entity in the world. Otherwise, his eyeballs would roll up and he would be in another state altogether. This was his way of bringing some grossness and inertia into his system, so that he could be like everybody else for some time. Otherwise, it is possible his system would have vaporized into thin air. Many yogis have, over the centuries, adopted this strategy: they deliberately use certain substances in order to retain their physical bodies.

Popular imagery of Adiyogi often shows him eating from a human skull. That was his soup bowl – a reminder that he was not invested in the transience of the flesh but in an intelligence far above it, not in the body but in the beyond, not in the corporeal but in consciousness. If you look at the entire cosmos as an organism, the brain, or the seat of intelligence, would be the Creator. This is the choice that Adiyogi exercised, and this is the possibility that yoga represents – complete freedom from the compulsiveness of the physical.

Adiyogi's varied approaches as a teacher testify to the fact that spiritual transmission is never based on the likes and dislikes of the guru. The teaching is always on the basis of the disciple's receptivity. For Adiyogi, who was in a constant state of ecstasy, none of this was work; whatever he did was and still is just an outpouring of his bliss. He offers it freely to whoever seeks it.

There were three fundamental approaches that he adopted. To one person, he said, 'Come, sit on my lap.' To the seven sages, he gave an extraordinarily intricate exposition about the mechanics and possibilities of the human system and cosmic nature. To the Ganas, he simply said, 'Drink of me and dance.'

Or, to put it another way, he told Parvati, 'There is no distance between you and enlightenment.' To the sages, he said, 'There is an infinite distance between you and enlightenment.' To the Ganas, he said, 'There *is* no enlightenment.'

What do these diverse utterances mean? Are they as contrary as they sound?

They are not. Each of Adiyogi's articulations was based on the disciple's need and present level of understanding. These approaches became the basis of three significant modes of delivery and, over the millennia, these took on many different forms.

Each of the three approaches that Adiyogi offered is important. What he imparted to the sages has lived this long because it is a clear methodology. What he imparted to Parvati was just an embrace. She knew what she needed to know, but this could not be transmitted over a period of time. It would never have lived over fifteen thousand years. It would be just a story, and it would not have the power to transform others.

For those who are willing to break out of the shell of their individuality, however, this possibility is still very much alive. Many women sages down the ages, from Andal to Akka Mahadevi and Meera, have walked the path of passionate intimacy with the divine. So have many men.

The seven sages did not have a burst of experience, but they steadily built themselves to a place from where there was no coming back. Parvati had momentary spurts of ecstasy, but when she came down from her exalted states, she had her problems. The process was quicker for her because it was a gift. The sages worked towards it. With her, Adiyogi used his intimacy; with them, he used the intellect.

With the Ganas, he used neither. He dismissed both. They did not need to be embraced and they did not need to work for it. They simply knew they were parts of him, and they did not ask for more.

No single approach was superior or inferior to the other; each was according to the requirements of the disciple.

Adiyogi never offered any of his disciples a belief system. The one common aspect of his approach with all three of them was his insistence that they be seekers rather than believers, exuberantly confused rather than dogmatically certain. He did not exhort his disciples to passive worship or prayer. He invited them, instead, to dynamic participation: to walk with him, to debate with him, to explore with him, to drink of him, to become one with him.

The Adiyogi story is not meant to lead us to conclusions. It is meant to lead us to a state that is alive, exploratory and responsive to the deepening mysteries of existence. It is an invitation from certainty to consciousness, from religiosity to responsibility, from the rigidity of logic to the roaring ecstasy of life itself.

THE DANCE OF LIGHT

In the eternal stillness of 'that which is not', as the first throb of energy began to reverberate, a new dance came into being. This was the first dance of the cosmos. A tremendous kinetic explosion of energy and ecstasy.

Modern science tells us that if electromagnetic energy is applied to a vacuum, subatomic particles will manifest and begin to dance. In the yogic tradition, this dance, self-generated from utter stillness, has been called the dance of creation. It has given rise to one of the most significant images of Adiyogi – that of Nataraja, the dancer whose stage is the cosmos, whose dance is the simultaneous creation and destruction of entire universes. In this performance without beginning or end, the dancer is the dance, and the performer and the witness indissolubly united.

In the East, divinity has always been synonymous with dance. Shiva's cosmic dance, in all its grace, vigour and splendour, is symbolic of life at peak performance. Dance is also seen as one of the most blissful paths of self-dissolution for a spiritual seeker.

Lore records many occasions on which Adiyogi danced. He performed for the pleasure of his wife, Parvati, on Mount Kailash one evening, to the accompaniment of a celestial choir of musicians. He is also known as the frenzied dancer of destruction around the burning pyres of cremation grounds – an image that invokes him as a complex emblem of death and new life all at once.

However, the place that enshrines him most memorably is a temple town in south India named Chidambaram. Nataraja here has assumed iconic status for his ananda tandava, or dance of eternal bliss, immortalized by the great sculptors of the south. Here Nataraja's dance represents the yogic ideal. It is seen as a spellbinding confluence of effervescence and stillness, exuberance and equanimity.

It happened...

One day, Adiyogi walked into a cedar forest in the Himalayas. He was in a heightened state of arousal where his energies had hit their peak on all 114 chakras. Clad in nothing but a garland of forest flowers, in a state of nirkaya or complete unawareness of the body, he walked in naked splendour into a forest hermitage.

The sages of the forest were busy with their meditations. But their wives, mothers, sisters and daughters were entranced by the beautiful presence of this mendicant. They flocked around him, unable to conceal their fascination with his radiant form and utter lack of self-consciousness. They followed him, unable to leave his side.

Each responded to him in her own way, but none could stay away from him. Drawn to him like ants to honey, some were entranced by the sweetness of his presence, while others touched him and went instantly into states of delirious ecstasy, and still others threw decorum to the wind and climbed upon his sturdy, tree-trunk-like body to savour him. They drank deep of his ecstasy through their eyes, ears, tongues and fingertips, through every pore in their bodies, and in every possible way.

For this was the essential nature of Adiyogi. He was existence untamed, a wild raging torrent of life itself –utterly without self-consciousness or pretention, capable of taking those around him into primal states of abandon and self-forgetfulness.

When the sages emerged from their practices, they found themselves irresistibly drawn to this strange figure as well, for the effulgence of his energies was beyond all dualities. But they were more than a little perturbed at the effect the beggar seemed to be having on the women in their lives.

They remonstrated with him, pleading that his abandon and lack of propriety would wreck their homes and families. 'You must do something,' they said. 'You walk around naked, unconcerned about the effect you have on others. You are disruptive. You wreck the norms on which our societies rest, the foundations on which our families and clans are rooted, the values on which all civilization is based. Our daughters, wives and mothers have lost all sense of age, decorum, dignity and social standing. Grand as your presence is, it unleashes anarchy. Where will this lead?'

Adiyogi heard them and then roared in laughter. It was a roar that shook the very foundations on which human culture is based – a culture that does its best to create a fragile, provisional order out of the great wilderness and inspired chaos of nature.

He took a sword from one of the sages and, without a moment's hesitation, severed his phallus. It dropped to the ground and became a radiant shaft of energy and light. This flaming shaft pierced the entire cosmos, uniting this world to the beyond through the limitless dimensions of space and time. This column of fire came to be called the linga – the sacred form – revered thereafter as a symbol of eternal life.

Continuing to roar in laughter, Adiyogi pointed towards the trajectory of this shaft, indicating that the ultimate order of creation is the only real order, the final and unfailing refuge of every creature in existence. The puny and fallible orders that are a fallout of human intellect and emotion will invariably turn into narrow prisons of limitation and bondage. Ultimate freedom, he indicated, is only in bringing life to its pristine and unbounded state of natural effulgence.

Adiyogi's laughter reverberated through the farthest reaches of the universe and then transformed itself into a rapturous dance. As the cosmic dancer, Nataraja, he exploded into a dance of triumph over the forces of darkness and ignorance, greed and folly, a dance witnessed in rapt amazement by all the sages and the gods in their celestial realms.

Later, to fulfil the wish of one of his cherished devotees, Adiyogi agreed to perform his great dance of mystical ecstasy once again at the sacred site of Thillai or Chidambaram, considered to be the very centre of the world.

What makes Chidambaram so sacred in the yogic tradition?

Chidambaram is derived from the word 'chitta', a dimension of intelligence unsullied by memory. In consciously touching that intelligence, the seeker also enters the dimension of limitless space or 'ambara'.

At the time of its construction, the Chidambaram temple was located exactly on the magnetic equator (which has since shifted). At the magnetic equator (which is distinct from the geographic equator), the zero degree of magnetic play helps promote a certain balance and alignment in the lives of those who choose to pursue their spiritual lives there. Additionally, Chidambaram is located on eleven degrees north latitude. The tilt of the planet at this latitude impels centrifugal forces in a nearly vertical direction which, in turn, pushes energy upward through the human physiological system.

The convergence of the magnetic equator with this latitude offered natural assistance for both equanimity and the ascent of human energy – an ideal blend for those seeking to liberate themselves from the physical.

When intensity meets relaxation, it is considered to be the ultimate blend for a spiritual seeker. The problem with most seekers, however, is that they confuse intensity with tension, and relaxation with laxity. To achieve a balance of these seemingly opposite states is a fine art that is achieved after arduous yogic practice.

This is the combination that Nataraja embodies – intensity and relaxation, exuberance and equanimity, dynamism and stillness, creation and dissolution, ecstatic movement and supreme awareness, samadhi and pragna, in flawless and unerring equipoise.

MAINSTREAMING TRUTH

A stout atheist once announced to me, upon introduction, 'Do you know that I believe there is no God?'

I replied, 'Really? I don't believe even that!'

That freedom to believe or not to believe is one of the tremendous contributions of Adiyogi to the spiritual culture of the world. He gave us another choice, a deeper choice. He gave us the choice to remain as we are, a puppet of unconscious instincts and unresolved psychological demons, or to grow into our ultimate possibility, our birthright: the condition of divinity.

While he is venerated as Pashupati and Vrikshanatha, the compassionate protector of all animal and vegetal forms of life, he is significant to humankind as Adiyogi, the one who offered yoga, a science of self-understanding that enabled us to use all the resources at our command – our bodies, our minds, our hearts, and our energies – to uncover our authentic nature.

And what is that authentic nature?

A state of absolute oneness with the fundamental state that precedes all physical manifestation and mental modification. A state of abiding union with 'that which is not', the basis of all existence.

Externally, we may be differently endowed in terms of physical ability, intelligence and capability; internally, however, there are no such distinctions. The possibility of attaining our ultimate nature, therefore, is open to everyone, irrespective of class, caste, creed or gender. It is a telling comment on Adiyogi that his disciples included a woman and a band of social outcasts. He was the first to demonstrate that the spiritual journey bars none.

When Adiyogi told the seven sages to preserve the integrity of the seed of yoga, he clearly envisioned a planet that would at one point turn collectively to this science. 'Your business is not to teach yoga to everybody; your business is to keep the potency of the seed,' he told them. 'You keep the seed pure and strong. When the climate is right, it will happen.'

The climate seems to be right for yoga in the world today. For the first time, the entire planet is aware of the term. Whether people are yet practising it or not, they know that the word 'yoga' exists. This could well be the turning point, the beginning of an era that Adiyogi had envisaged many thousands of years ago.

Other than Parvati and his Ganas, Adiyogi found only seven disciples in his time. Even those seven needed years of preparation. For a being of his stature, seven disciples are an absurdly small number. Centuries later, the effort of my life is to see that he finds many more to walk his path, because in the history of humanity, a being like that has come only once. His shadows have come, his reflections have come. But only one like him has ever walked this planet.

Many great beings have come and gone. They have kept aspects of his wisdom alive. They have, however, always been on the fringe. For the first time, thanks to information technology and systems of communication on this planet, there is the possibility of truth turning mainstream.

For far too long on this planet, in a variety of ways, authority has masqueraded as truth. To this very day Adiyogi stands testimony to the fact that truth is the only authority.

PART THREE

DIALOGUES

ARUNDHATHI SUBRAMANIAM

'WHEN THE MARKET IS RIGHT'

While I enjoy listening to Sadhguru's retelling of the Adiyogi saga – with all its rhythms and tides, crests and eddies – there are questions that linger.

Questions about Adiyogi. Questions about Sadhguru. Questions about how all this links to every seeker's fundamental questions about life and how to live it.

This section is a series of excerpts of conversations with Sadhguru: one that happened in the yoga centre in Coimbatore and the others on a journey to Mount Kailash. They offer a glimpse of what it was like to be around as this book unfolded – not as a linear narrative, but as a labyrinth of anecdotes and digressions, insights and parentheses. Spontaneous, freewheeling, abrupt, enigmatic, Sadhguru's verbal style is distinct. He circles a subject, swerves away, and suddenly returns to the point from another angle altogether.

This is an invitation to the reader to draw close to the campfire. It is an invitation to eavesdrop on the broken, informal rhythms of conversation. It is an invitation to intimacy.

I am sitting with Sadhguru in what is called the Adiyogi Alayam Room at the Isha Yoga Centre. Sadhguru has decided to set aside a day for a conversation on Adiyogi – a momentous occurrence in his frenzied schedule. I'm not sure what it means. But I know it is significant.

I am usually prepared to ambush him with a flurry of questions. But today, I decide to pursue a single line of enquiry. It is about motivation. Why has Sadhguru, the stout proponent of yoga as a science of human well-being, turned raconteur? Why has the inner engineer turned folklorist? Is Sadhguru suddenly turning traditionalist?

'What's the big deal about Adiyogi? Is that what you're asking?' Sadhguru laughs.

I suppose I am.

'All we are doing today is offering a simpler expression of that incredibly sophisticated science that he gave us without dumbing it down. Right now, you don't understand how the telecommunication system works. But you have learnt how to use it. To figure the electromagnetic forces it takes an Einstein. But you know how to use the end product, the telephone. That is all we are doing with Adiyogi. We are just making the hugely sophisticated science he gave us into a user-friendly system. That is why I speak of technologies of well-being. To benefit, this is all you need. But to discover a science, to be able to explore the algorithms of the human mechanism, you need a different level of capability altogether. That deserves to be acknowledged. Why? Because there is no system of human self-understanding more extensive than this.'

'But every faith makes claims of supremacy for its founder,' I begin.

'This has nothing to do with religion,' Sadhguru is definitive. 'This predates all religion. It happened before the idea of religion entered the human mind. Adiyogi offered us a science. That is why it is important. Anyone can take to it. It doesn't take belief and it doesn't take faith. It is not a teaching. It is one hundred per cent experiential.'

'But why can't we invoke him in his more abstract representation – as a linga?' I ask.

My bafflement at this point is less about Adiyogi and more about Sadhguru. Why this need to invoke the historical Adiyogi? After all, as the author of the Dhyanalinga, Sadhguru has a refined understanding of the science of linga-making with all its arcane nuances. He has often discussed how the legacy of the seven sages can be found in ancient sacred sites around the world. Many of the menhirs and megaliths, he explains, are lingas with one or two consecrated chakras (invariably to promote health, well-being or material prosperity). The unique feature of the Dhyanalinga, however, is that it embodies all seven dimensions, capable of addressing every human desire from well-being to liberation. It is Shiva as the ultimate teacher, in fact.

Sadhguru once traced the origin of this project to a moment in remote antiquity. 'Thousands of years ago, in the Himalayas, in modern-day Nepal, there lived a yogi named Sunira. He lived a couple of generations after Adiyogi. Memories of Adiyogi must still have been vivid. People must have been missing him. So Sunira initiated this project of creating an absolutely perfect being. He tried to create a world teacher by synthesizing all the dimensions of human existence, a teacher capable of planting the seeds of consciousness for the benefit of the entire world.'

Sunira did his best, but apparently failed. Before he died, however, he made a prophecy: 'One day, the perfect being will exist. He will take shape amid the green hills of southern Jambudvipa (the ancient name for the Indian subcontinent). And then he will reach the world.'

Sunira died. But the project endured. Several yogis took up the project. Each of them was compelled to concede failure. The perfect being, the ideal master, who never quite materialized, came to be called Maitreya, the Universal Friend. But Maitreya remained an unfinished master. 'Many mystics added substance to him,' said Sadhguru, 'but he was never completed.'

And yet, 'another kind of intelligence', in Sadhguru's words, was brought to the Maitreya project by southern Indian mysticism. 'People always thought a perfect being would walk the world and teach. But he doesn't have to. There are other ways in which transmission can happen.'

The yogis of the south aspired to create another kind of spiritual guide – not a Maitreya of flesh and blood, but equally alive, equally potent, equally powerful, and more enduring. They called this form the Dhyanalinga.

Sadhguru's personal life story seems to have entered this ancient narrative through a strange mix of happenstance and grace. Looking back, the saga seems to unfold as a tapestry of superlative design and inevitability. After lifetimes of failure, the Dhyanalinga stands tall today – a yogic feat that offers the possibility of liberation for all.

It also seems to make Sunira's prophecy about the perfect world master ring uncannily true. As Sadhguru says with a laugh, 'We *are* in the south, and the hills are green…'

And yet, this world master is obviously quite different from that envisaged by Sunira. 'The Dhyanalinga sits in one place and transmits,' says Sadhguru. 'He won't walk; he won't teach; he just transmits. But transmission is, in the long run, much more important than teaching. Teaching is only a way of knocking on the door. All gurus transmit – and anyway, all yogis are meant to sit! The Dhyanalinga does both. He is a perfect being without the frailties of being human.'

This brings me back to my primary question. Why was an adept of the highest calibre – one who understood Shiva as the ultimate technology of transformation – now talking about a yogi who lived many thousand years ago? And, for the rest of us, didn't the real beauty of Shiva lie in myth, in iconography, in the human imagination? Why was Sadhguru turning metaphor into fact? Why was he literalizing legend?

I put the question bluntly. 'Why are you invoking Adiyogi as history? Indian culture has always been comfortable with metaphor. Isn't that its strength?'

Sadhguru laughs. 'It is.'

I persist. 'When the Tamil poets of medieval south India sing of Shiva, for instance, they see him as intensely local – the god who lives down the street right now, rather than someone who lived in a remote Himalayan mountain millennia ago. Why is it necessary to see Adiyogi as a historical figure? Why can't we celebrate him as myth?'

Sadhguru's reply is swift. 'He did live down their street. And he did live in the Himalayas. Both are true.'

'What does that mean?'

'The mystical dimension should not be separated from reality as we know it. It is very important that the two remain linked. Otherwise, Adiyogi will become just another fanciful story.'

'And it's not?'

'It's not,' he asserts forcefully. 'Mysticism was explored *on this planet*. It did not happen in a vacuum. For us to recognize its importance, it needs an ecosystem that supports it and is supported by it.

'Just believing a story isn't enough. We need to be able to see its impact, how it transforms people. Only then we can see how connected it is to our lives. And that's why it is important to see Adiyogi not just as myth but as fact. Not just as a divine being but as a yogi.'

'And both are true?'

'Both are true. Both are important.'

'But when you say Adiyogi came from Kailasa, how are we to understand this? Do you mean he came from another dimension altogether?'

Sadhguru laughs. 'I'd rather not talk about this. I have a reputation as a straight-shooting guru!' After a long pause, he says reflectively, 'I have been digging into what tradition says about him. One recurrent description is that he was a Yakshaswaroopa. That means he was a celestial being; he did not belong here. We hear a lot about him, but we never hear of his parentage, his old age, or his death, as we do in the case of other figures like Rama or Krishna. He was clearly capable of assuming a human form when required – sometimes that went well, sometimes not so well.'

'Are you suggesting that he was –', I am a bit awkward about using the word, but I go ahead anyway, 'extraterrestrial?' (My unstated question is still sheer puzzlement: 'We're trying to come to terms with an existential Shiva, a metaphysical Shiva, an anthropomorphic Shiva, and even a technological Shiva; are you now adding an *alien* Shiva to the mix?')

Sadhguru laughs. 'When you label someone "extraterrestrial", you are drawing a conclusion. A simplistic conclusion.

'Do you know where *you* came from? When Adiyogi said the whole universe can be packed into a mustard seed, who is extraterrestrial and who is not?

'Adiyogi was the first to say that all of creation is just a play of five elements. If you understand these five, you have understood the nature and mechanics of life. Human bodies have a particular composition of elements; similarly, there is a different compositional formula for every species on the planet, and likewise for any being in any part of the universe.

'So who belongs and who doesn't? Only a rudimentary mind divides everything. Geographical divisions, planetary divisions, galactic divisions don't exist. Creation is one big happening. It is only the intellect that tries to fragment it.

'When we say "Shiva" we are talking about a dimension beyond the five elements. Forms can be adopted and discarded. That is all human life is anyway. Forms happen and they vanish. They are just pop-ups. That is all we are.

'The word for celestial in today's language, is extraterrestrial – or "alien". The Americans have taken this word a little too far, though; the immigration counters describe even me as an "alien"!' He laughs. 'So, I am from the other side too. I came with an alien permit, you know?'

'But how exactly do we understand Adiyogi then?' I ask. 'Could he be considered an *avatar*?'

There is a long silence.

'Whenever the need arises, consciousness will centralize in the form of a person or a whole lot of people,' Sadhguru says finally. 'In the *Bhagavad Gita*, Krishna is supposed to have said, "Whenever there is a need, I will manifest." He is not referring to himself as a person. He is referring to himself as a limitless consciousness which will manifest naturally when needed. *That* is an avatar.

'In times of strife, a certain percentage of people will start looking for a solution. The questions will arise: "What's all this about? Why this mess? Why can't we go beyond this?" When that thought enters many minds, consciousness will manifest. Ultimately, the solution for every issue in the universe is consciousness. If it manifests as a single figure, that becomes a fulcrum for all these other forces and people to gather and function. So, such an individual who becomes a fulcrum gets referred to as an avatar. Individuals are only an embodiment, but it is just a single consciousness at work. A single consciousness becomes incarnate.

'If people were extremely perceptive, there would be no need for embodiment. But, otherwise, somebody's voice has to be heard. That voice might emerge sometimes from an individual, but it is actually more of a centralized expression of a certain ferment that is happening all over the place.

'Right now, this upsurge of yoga here in southern India may seem to be centralized in me. But it is not just me. That longing is there all over the region. Otherwise, it wouldn't succeed.

'My sitting here and talking about Adiyogi as the source of yoga, for instance, is not delinked from some scientist in Harvard saying, "Yoga definitely works." They are connected. It is happening because there is a certain global churning in that direction. When that churning finds a voice, we might call it an avatar.

'When we want to reinstate Adiyogi today as an iconic figure, it is to once again give a voice, an embodiment to the silent revolution happening all over the world. Anyway, all the New-Age people are talking about the rise in consciousness, aren't they?' Sadhguru laughs. 'Whether they know what they're talking about or not, this is a good time for us to work at raising it! When so many people believe that consciousness is going to rise, it *will* rise. When human beings believe something is going to work, they will move in that direction. They want to move towards success, not failure. After all, who doesn't want to vote for a winning party?

'So, what Krishna is saying in the Gita, to put it crudely, is that when the market is right, we will release the product! That's exactly what we're doing.'

I'm not sure I've got my answer. But we break for lunch.

Later, the conversation turns to matters cosmological. 'There are traditions in which the female principle, the Divine Mother, is presented as the origin of the universe,' I remark. 'Why these contrary versions?'

Sadhguru chuckles. 'All the creation myths tell us that the universe emerged from a single source. That is all that counts. These gender divisions exist only in your mind, not in reality.

'Yes, there are these many different stories in the lore. See, devotees have the freedom to create the metaphors they want, and interpret the lore whichever way they want. But, unfortunately, even scholars have taken that freedom; they should not. Once you approach this with the intellect, you'll miss the point of the story altogether.

'Devotees have a certain freedom – the way it works for them, that's how they make the story. They are not making a statement of fact. They are just getting the system to work for them.'

I see the point. I know the dangers of literalizing metaphor. I know the dangers of turning mythology into ideology. It's just that I'm sometimes baffled by the way Sadhguru segues between legend and history. I return to the story of Adiyogi which seems to present its own share of paradoxes. 'Adiyogi seems to have been capable of aloofness and engagement, stillness and dynamism. Lots of seeming contradictions there too. Is that also metaphor?'

'No. No contradictions there.' Sadhguru is emphatic. 'You either participate in life out of your compulsions or out of your consciousness. Consciousness means to be beyond compulsiveness. Compulsiveness means repetitive nature. Adiyogi participates out of consciousness. He recognizes that there are compulsions in people, but the whole spiritual process is to rise beyond that.

'Adiyogi's life is about freedom. If he wishes to involve himself, he can. But he is not compelled by anything. He is not a compulsive thinker. He is not a compulsive physical body. He is not compulsive about his emotions. If he wishes to, he can engage in all these areas; if he does not wish to, he will not.'

'But he seems to have been a reluctant householder,' I interject.

'People think being conscious, non-compulsive is not engaging with life. That is because they're living in samsara, which is cyclical existence. If somebody is not in a cyclical mode, they think he is not interested in life. But a conscious person can engage with life with much greater involvement than anyone else when he wishes to.

'The problem is that people are celebrating their compulsions. Do you want to celebrate your compulsions, or do you want to obliterate your compulsions? That is the basic question.

'It is a question most people are not willing to address within themselves. If they addressed this one question genuinely, everything would be settled. But it doesn't matter how many times they are reminded, they will not address this, because it is their nemesis as individuals. It is self-annihilation. Even after they die, they want to exist somewhere else!'

'But isn't it gloomy – the premise about human existence being bondage?' I ask. 'Isn't this often seen as Eastern pessimism, this idea that life is maya, relative reality; that it is samsara, cyclical reality? Do we really want to be free of it? Is liberation what we're really seeking? What's so wrong with samsara?'

'Nothing wrong,' Sadhguru asserts. 'But it's limited, isn't it? Limited between the parallel lines of birth and death. Human intelligence naturally dislikes limitations. So, the longing to go beyond is a natural longing. Adiyogi just explored ways to fulfil that longing. All he is saying is, here are ways to get out of those limitations, if you want to.

'If you want to celebrate your psychological reality, go ahead. I'm sure people have parties in their prison cells too! There's nothing wrong with that. When you're trapped, it's good to make the best of it. But once you make it pleasant for yourself, there is a natural longing for something more, that's all. When life is pleasant, when everything is working the way you want, there is invariably an enthusiasm and energy to explore life beyond this psychological bubble. If it is unpleasant, dealing with that unpleasantness will itself keep you busy for a lifetime or more.

'Unlike your psychological reality, which is of your making, existential reality is not of your making. It will exist even if you don't. So it is very natural to want to find something which will endure even if you don't, because that is your true security, your stability. That is your freedom.'

'What does it mean exactly to be a conscious thinker as opposed to a compulsive one?' I ask.

'Consciousness means you move into a different dimension every moment.'

'Yes, but what does that mean *experientially*? As an enlightened being, what is your experience?'

Sadhguru pauses. 'At this moment, I have twelve to fourteen independent tracks or channels of activity running in my mind,' he says at length. 'That is how it is within me all the time, but it doesn't distract me in any way from what I'm doing. That may sound crazy, but it's true.'

'Is that even possible?' I ask doubtfully.

'That's what consciousness means. Right now, you're in a compulsive state of thought. If one thought enters your mind, it gets you tangled up. If you're in a conscious state, you can run any number of tracks in your mind. Because it's not compulsive, it doesn't entangle you.

'So compulsiveness takes away the possibility of exploring the full depth and dimension of life; it prevents you from realizing its immensity. In a state of consciousness, you can carry this mind with you without becoming a part of it.

'See, there are only two ways to live life. You can impart your qualities upon the material that you gather, or you can take on the qualities of the material that you gather. That is the fundamental choice you have. That is yoga.

'That is tantra too in its present conceptualization: whatever is drawing you into a vortex of cyclic compulsiveness, you can use that in a reverse way to get out of it.'

'So what exactly was the basis of the tantric approach that Adiyogi adopted with Parvati?'

'You must remember first that tantra is not a separate path; it is a branch of yoga,' says Sadhguru. 'The word "yoga" means union. A yogi is someone who has come from the experience of that union with existence. Tantra means technology. A tantrik is someone who has some mastery over a particular technology. So, tantra is a consequence of yoga.

'The basic principle is that the very things that can be your downfall in life can be used to raise yourself. If you simply change your perspective, what is down can be up. What is a downward chute can be used as an upward process. Whatever draws you into compulsive nature, you use that to become conscious. You use that momentum to grow.

'But today, there is a misconception about tantra. Many think it means unbridled promiscuity. You must understand that actual tantra involves an enormous amount of discipline. It is about being in conscious proximity with sexuality, or food, or intoxicants, but not getting entangled with them. And if it is not done under proper guidance, you will only become trapped in those compulsions; you will not be able to come out of them.

'Food, sex and intoxicants are vortices that draw most people towards a certain limitation; they represent things that people are compulsive about. What people are compulsive about can be approached consciously. Whatever draws you compulsively traps you; but if you approach it consciously, you can evolve beyond it. This is the principal premise of tantra. But it remains a more rudimentary approach than yoga. Yoga is highly refined, highly internal.

'You've heard of two broad varieties of tantra: left hand and right hand. Left-hand tantra uses more outside material; right-hand tantra uses less. With yoga, no external material is used whatsoever.'

'What about the many questions Parvati asked Adiyogi?' I ask. 'Dialogue seems to have been an important mode, a significant part of the spiritual process.'

'The culture of debate is characteristic of this land,' declares Sadhguru. 'One that we definitely should not lose. This is a spiritual culture of seekers, not believers; of quest, not commandment. Here what is considered to be religious or sacred can be *debated*. It does not have to be obeyed. In this land, there is no concept of sacrilege. Everything can be turned into the sacred.

'Human beings have a fundamental longing to know. Only the spirit of questioning will quench this longing. The spiritual history of this land has long recognized this fact. Even when entities that we considered divine appeared in this land, we did not simply obey them. We debated with them. We bombarded them with questions! We recognized that they represented an opportunity for us to turn from believers into seekers.

'What happened between Shiva and Parvati was a spirited conversation, conducted in the deepest intimacy between husband and wife. Later, an equally celebrated dialogue took place between Krishna and Arjuna on the battlefield. One happened in a situation of intimacy, the other on the brink of extreme violence. But, either way, the presence of a divine entity is always seen as a tremendous opportunity to ask questions of ultimate import, not an occasion to settle for mere solace.'

Since we are on the subject of Parvati, I decide to deepen the question of Adiyogi's pedagogical approaches. 'From the Adiyogi story, some might conclude that the spiritual path for women is necessarily the way of the heart (as it was for Parvati) and for men, the way of the intellect (as it was for the sages).'

'It would be absolutely wrong to draw such a conclusion,' Sadhguru shakes his head. Often, in the past, social variables, shaped by biological factors, determined the spiritual path adopted by individuals. If you pursued the path of gnana or the intellect, it would take years and years of committed, single-minded practice. In traditional societies, such an option was largely unacceptable for women. So, the quicker way was often the path of the heart.

In today's world, where much has been levelled out by technology, these distinctions don't count.

'But there have been women of prodigious intellect who have walked the spiritual path; Maitreyi and Gargi are the celebrated examples in this subcontinent. There have also been many men who have walked the path of the heart. These include the devotional saints – Appar, Sundarar, Tukaram, Surdas, Chaitanya, Tulsidas, to name just a few.

'Adiyogi's three approaches were based on the disciples he had around him. It would be misleading to extrapolate, based on that. In fact, what makes yoga such a complete science is that it offers a path for individuals of every orientation and context.'

'What about the role of belief in a seeker's life?' I ask. 'This culture also believes in a wonderful assortment of gods and goddesses, doesn't it?'

'Belief in this culture was seen as a psychological process, but never a substitute for knowing. Belief was not seen in opposition to reason because you adopted a belief, knowing fully well that belief was yours and may have nothing to do with reality, and may find no concurrence with anyone around you.

'This is why in the same home, five family members can pray to five different gods, without any friction or discord. There is no perceived dichotomy because gods are seen as devices. You always had the freedom to create as many as you desired. But belief offered temporary solace until you found the strength to seek the truth for yourself. Whenever great beings appeared, we became seekers. Until then, we believed.

'There are accounts of colourful and vigorous debates between disciples and masters down the centuries. Even those beings who were seen as avatars or embodiments of divinity were subjected to gruelling questions. This tradition can be traced all the way back to that historic dialogue between Parvati and Adiyogi. The cultural memory of fifteen thousand years still lives on!'

I turn to the story of the seven sages – those men of fierce determination and intellect – with whom Adiyogi chose to adopt the yogic rather than the tantric model. 'Several people were drawn to Adiyogi's presence,' I point out. 'Why did only seven remain?'

'Yes, thousands came with the same thirst, but only seven organized their thirst into proper seeking. This is true everywhere. It is the case even today.'

'Why?'

'For example, thousands of people come to me, but only a few will organize their thirst into a purposeful process. Others will come, have a few experiences, and they will go.

'This happens for various reasons. One is that they may not have the necessary *samskriti* or tradition behind them. They may not have the necessary *samskara* – past impressions – within them. They may not have the karmic impetus within them, or the necessary cultural atmosphere, psychological balance or economic situation.

'They may have gotten trapped. They may already have a thirty-year mortgage on their house! Whatever. To go beyond all that and make a decision – "This is what I want to do" – takes a certain culturing of the mind. Otherwise, the mind has a thousand distractions to follow.

'It needs a certain streak of intensity beyond sense and sanity to seek the ultimate. Because what you label as sense or sanity are just the limits you set upon yourself. Even those who get spoonfuls of spirituality find that their lives get enhanced – their health, their relationships improve dramatically. But the intensity of their longing is such that it gets satisfied with small fulfilments.'

'And what about linga? Was that also an esoteric legacy that Adiyogi imparted to the sages?'

I know we're moving towards a subject dear to Sadhguru. Consecration is his métier, the domain in which he is clearly a virtuoso. As he once said, 'If there's one thing I'm really good at, it's making a place crackle with energy.'

For those who have witnessed his ability to transform spaces, there is little doubt that he is an alchemist of no mean calibre. When I was once on a car ride with him, I asked him what kind of 'energy information' he could pick up about his environment. He replied that he could know right away if there had been a death in the vicinity. 'And if there is a shrine that has been powerfully consecrated nearby, I would know that too,' he added.

He now seems to be musing aloud. 'Linga-making became a very deep science in the Indian subcontinent. But as a form, the linga is not found only here. Almost everywhere in the world there are lingas. In Africa, there is a variety of terracotta lingas used for occult purposes. The native Americans in South America have used lingas for similar purposes in a different context. In Europe there used to be many lingas before the Inquisition. One which has survived is in Delphi, Greece – referred to as the "Navel of the Earth". When I saw it, it was clear to me that this was consecrated about four thousand years ago by Indian yogis. It is a distillation of the manipura chakra which is the dimension of maintenance, wealth and prosperity. It has remained intact, but now they have moved it from its original place to a museum.

'Some of the African lingas are in American museums today. What used to be established in a certain type of temple, people dug out and took to their museums because they found them interesting archaeological relics and thought them to be phallic symbols. What was never known is that these are energized forms, powerful forms, created with a definite purpose. There are, in fact, different kinds of lingas, created for a whole variety of purposes – from personal protection to material well-being.

'It seems very likely that this science was carried by the seven sages to these parts of the world. But much more research needs to be done in this area.'

'For many, consecration seems like a kind of magic,' I remark.

'It is a science. A science of transformation,' says Sadhguru emphatically. 'We are surrounded by transformation all the time, but we forget to notice this everyday magic – the magic of agriculture (transforming earth into food), of digestion (transforming food into flesh), of death (transforming flesh into earth). Consecration is just a process of making that everyday transformation conscious and purposeful.'

'So as his fifty per cent partner, you are the recipient of Adiyogi's knowing entirely through live spiritual transmission?' I ask.

Sadhguru nods. After a reflective pause, he says, 'When I say he is my partner, it is not an achievement. The word "Shi-va" suggests a certain inertness. "That which is not" has to find expression through more active manifestations of life. He has found various manifestations down the ages. And that is how he lives on. I consider it a fortune and privilege that he finds expression through me at this moment.'

'You do seem to have been a devotee in a previous lifetime,' I say, 'a devotee who would not accept the intervention of a guru unless he assumed the form of Shiva.'

Sadhguru laughs. 'Yes, that is the madness from which I come. It took a couple of lifetimes to be cured of Shiva.'

There is a long pause.

'Some time ago,' he says, 'someone asked me if I was a devotee of Adiyogi. I said, "I'm not a devotee of Adiyogi. What have I done for him? Do I pray to him every day? I do nothing for him. My devotion is not for Adiyogi."'

He shakes his head, incredulously: 'I told him, do you know what a guru means? My bloody devotion is not for Shiva. Is that so difficult to understand? It is for you. I took this birth to make it happen for you. Day in and day out, my life is for you.'

And I am back to the old Sadhguru paradox. This is the rational guru who demystifies spiritual traditions. But he is also the mystic who embodies their deepest mysteries.

THE KAILASH CONUNDRUM

For a long time I believed Kailash was a myth.

So when I heard you could actually get there, it sounded a bit like buying a ticket to the Garden of Eden. Or taking a cruise liner to Vaikunth. (Or, at the risk of belabouring the point, an airbus to Jannat.)

A bit absurd. Myths are meant to be myths. Ageless and remote. Upfront and close only when you want them to be. Of course, Kailash was sumptuous, as all good myths should be. Consider an ascetic, a dancer, a lover, a yogi all rolled into a single cocktail. If Kailash was the abode of this kind of man for all seasons, it was heady stuff. I could see that.

But it was, after all, a yarn. For the brilliance of its tropes, it couldn't be bettered. As a story with an understanding of life and death, it was matchless. It could only have been dreamed up by a visionary poet, or a whole pantheon of visionary poets. It was a superlative story. A sacred story.

But a story, for god's sake. Rich, glorious fiction, not fact.

I'm not sure when the realization dawned – the fact that Kailash was also a place. Not even in my teens, when I vaguely recall overhearing that the Chinese had reopened the pilgrimage route that had been closed for two decades. It was much later. And I remember a vague sense of anticlimax when I learnt the truth. It seemed disconcertingly literal – the fact that Shiva should have a pin code.

And yet, I have a healthy respect for literalism myself. Standing on a sub-blazed stretch of Greek soil in Mycenae, I felt deeply grateful to all who had made this happen (from Homer to my travel agent) – this molten contact with the immediacy of myth. And I've had my Kodak moments in Bodh Gaya and Galilee, in Ramana Maharishi's ashram in Tiruvannamalai and the Sultan Ahmet mosque in Istanbul. So yes, I am a collector of memories, a hunter-gatherer of celebrity autographs, if you will.

I know what it's like to be breathless and embarrassingly sticky-palmed. I know what it's like to wait in line for my personal brush with immortality. I know what it's like to desperately want the concrete over the abstract.

But literalism has its limits. I thought that was the big plus of my cultural inheritance. I've always prided myself on a faith that isn't dependent on geography. India, contradictions notwithstanding, understands metaphor. I don't really need to visit Ayodhya to make Rama mine. And I don't need to visit Vrindavan to visualize Krishna's delirious raas leela under a full moon.

Literalism can be fatiguing. A little like seeing a film after reading a beloved novel. Too many gaps filled, too many dots joined. And people can turn literal about anything. I've known those who could quote Keats and Kalidasa, but who never seemed to have *tasted* any of it.

You get the point. I'm literalist enough to want first-hand experience over second-hand wisdom. But I'm wary of losing the spirit in the letter.

I know pilgrimages can sometimes change your life. But the operative word is *sometimes*. What the *Lankavatara Sutra* calls the 'turning around in the seat of consciousness' doesn't come easy. Pilgrimages are meant to be that chance to 'turn around'. But more often than not, they're about standing around in queues and yearning to throttle your fellow pilgrims.

Better one's imaginary worlds. They're more satisfying and, in the long run, less delusional. Also less expensive. And they don't come with visa officials and smelly bathrooms.

And yet, Kailash existed. It seemed now to belong to a shadowy midpoint between earth and sky. A kind of halfway house. As if geography had made an uneasy truce with human aspiration. Too smoky, still, to be fact, but too undeniable, too big, too present, to be just another old wives' tale.

The stories began seeping in. The Hindu, Jain and Buddhist traditions, I learnt, saw it as Meru, the central axis of the world. Writer John Snelling called it the 'great surveyor's rod at the heart of things, by its very presence giving coherence and form to that which would otherwise be incoherent and formless. It has the power, in short, to make cosmos out of chaos.'

That sounded big. But there was more. Lama Anagarika Govinda, the Buddhist scholar, called it 'the centre of the "Roof of the World", the heart of the biggest temple, the seat of cosmic powers, the axis which connects the earth with the universe, the super-antenna for the inflow and outflow of the spiritual energies of our planet.'

I learnt that Jains considered it the sacred site where their first master, Rishabhadeva, attained liberation. A Buddhist tradition apparently held that if twelve self-realized beings congregated at Kailash, the historic Buddha would materialize. There were stories that linked the greatest Tibetan mystics – from Padmasambhava to Milarepa – to the region around Kailash.

The Bon tradition of Tibet termed it 'the nine-storeyed swastika mountain', 'water's flower' and 'mountain of sea water', and the Tibetans regarded it as Kang Rinpoche, jewel of the snows, the spiritual pinnacle of the planet. Others wondered if Kailash were

Shambhala, the world's hidden paradisial kingdom of wisdom that can only be perceived clairvoyantly. There was also the intriguing tradition of never climbing the mountain, seasoned with juicy stories of the misfortune that befell those who tried.

And then, in 2006, I heard Sadhguru on Kailash.

'Mount Kailash is considered to be the abode of Shiva himself. What does that mean? Why is this remote Himalayan mountain so significant?

'The stories are many. But from the mystical point of view, there is a single reason: it is significant because some of the greatest masters down history chose to deposit and preserve their work there.

'Most mystics on the planet have found very few with whom they could share their knowing. If they find some with whom they can share even one or two per cent of their work, they are fortunate. Most don't even get to do that.

'It is not easy always to prepare people to receive mystical knowledge. It takes receptivity, a certain opening up of perception. There are also social restrictions, which limit the work you can do with people around you. Then there are people's own individual problems – psychological and physiological limitations, karmic bondages. It is rare to be able to find one or two people who can receive everything you know. Very few masters have been that fortunate. The rest have had to work around social norms and individual limitations. Not even a small percentage of what they know actually gets transmitted or shared.

'So, most mystics have found rocks very receptive! At least rocks don't know how to resist or misinterpret. They don't know how to go about judging what's okay and what's not. Most masters usually chose to deposit their knowing in some space that is not too frequented by human beings, but which is, at the same time, accessible to the committed pilgrim.

'There are many places like this in the world, places rich in spiritual vibration, places that reverberate with immense mystical knowledge. The Velliangiri Mountains in southern India are such a space. But the ultimate is considered to be Kailash. And when you go there, you know why.

'Centuries ago, Shiva, the greatest yogi of all time, tried to download all that he knew. His knowing was prodigious. He chose seven people into whom to download this immense knowing. When he could not find another human being who could grasp all the dimensions that he embodied, he decided to merge into the mountain itself.

'Other mystics added to this incredible storehouse of knowing. From Adiyogi to the first Jain tirthankara, Rishabha, from two of the greatest figures in Buddhism, Manjushree and Avalokiteshwara, to the saints of the Tibetan Bon tradition – all their work is preserved here in a single location. All the seven dimensions of yoga, of knowing, the very mechanics of life, are preserved in one single place, in one source.

'And so this is the greatest mystical library on the planet. Not just a repository of information, but a living library, a laboratory of human consciousness. That enormity is Kailash.

'In terms of the volume and the variety that has been deposited here, there is no other place like it. Yes, in a way, Shiva does live there, because what is Shiva without his knowing? It is because of what he did that we value him. All that is valuable for us from his life is right there. In that sense, he is alive. In an energy form, he is alive – as are many great beings who have lived and walked this planet.

'I have been to many truly sacred places. I have met many powerful beings. When I bow down to them, I always bow a little less than I would to my guru. But when I see Kailash, I do what I have never done before. I bow down to it in exactly the same way that I would bow to my master.'

ON THE ROAD WITH
THE MYSTIC

We are driving from Zhangmu to Saga, the last major town on the southern route to Mount Kailash, the ostensible abode of Adiyogi. It will take us around six hours. I am in the car with Sadhguru. We have decided to use this opportunity to discuss a possible book on Adiyogi, but this is still at a nascent stage. In any case, this comes pretty close to my idea of the ideal situation: a guru who can't escape, and I in the vicinity with a tape recorder.

For many years, I have longed to have someone who could answer my questions, someone who came from inner experience rather than informed hearsay. With Sadhguru's arrival, I couldn't believe that I actually had access to a real, live mystic in my life.

My restlessness has abated since Sadhguru came into my life. But the questions haven't gone away. My spiritual path is, I decide, definitely more Indian than Chinese – more of a bumpy, potholed dirt track than a flawless freeway. And the roadblocks are far from over.

However, what struck me about Sadhguru from the very beginning was that he doesn't resent questions. His answers to my questions are often forthright – at times cryptic. That hasn't stopped me from asking them. There are times I welcome the abruptness. That gives me the right to make my questions as blunt as I choose.

I would like it to be otherwise, but dewy-eyed faith isn't my thing. There is growing trust, there is wonder, certainly, but there are also, most definitely, questions. The good thing is that no question is taboo with Sadhguru. While his patience may have worn thin, I appreciate that he has never stopped answering my queries.

More significantly, there have been times when he's answered the questions even before I've asked them. I still find that uncanny and I'm not sure I'm comfortable with it. Many have experienced this. 'That's because I answer the questioner, not the question,' he often remarks.

There are three others in the car: Arjun, the gentle Sherpa who serves as navigator, when necessary; Radhe, Sadhguru's daughter, young, wide-eyed and chirpy; and a soft-spoken senior Isha teacher, who magically anticipates the needs of every situation and pulls out every kind of snack one could desire from the inexhaustible reserves of her bag.

To call Sadhguru a fast driver is an understatement. He simply pulverizes the road he drives on. I have been car-sick in a drive with him in the past. Thankfully, this time there are no hairpin bends. Or, perhaps, it's just that we're all so grateful that there *are* roads, in the first place, that we don't notice the speed.

Tibet flashes by, a marked contrast to the lushness of the Nepalese countryside. It is minimalist, almost lunar – a geography of boulder and moraine, mountain and lake, snowdrift and scrub. It is as if the chill winds have blasted away everything potentially decorative, and left behind only bone: pure, craggy, attenuated. The tones are smudgy grey, brown, muted green. Can any landscape really be so severely anti-baroque, I wonder, so devoid of even a hint of visual indulgence? So skeletal in its austerity? This feels like it could be a planet in its prenatal state, still blind in the womb.

In the distance, you see a herd of yaks, a lone tent, a solitary traveller (a monk? a herdsman? a trader?), and you know you could be witness to a scene from centuries ago. Not much seems to have changed in this cold, windswept land. And yet, of course, so much has. The roads, for one. Obviously, these are recent developments; they are almost birthing under our wheels as we drive.

'None of these were around even two years ago,' Sadhguru marvels.

While I'm grateful for them, he is clearly disappointed. The journey is getting too easy. There will come a time, he says, when Kailash will become a picnic spot, not a pilgrimage site.

'Is that a problem?' I ask. 'What if someone goes there as a tourist rather than a pilgrim? Does she miss out on something?'

'It takes openness to experience something,' he says briefly. 'A tourist won't necessarily approach it with that openness. But it is possible to be influenced by something even if you aren't aware of it. Many realize the significance of it later – sometimes even a lifetime later. That's why people have traditionally made the pilgrimage saying, even if it's not in this lifetime, let me acquire some merit at least for the next.'

'So what does a mountain as a mystical library really mean?'

'A library isn't just a heap of books,' Sadhguru says. 'It is a repository of knowledge. And this mountain just throbs with it. The volume of that knowledge is so large, it's unbelievable.'

'What kind of knowledge?'

'Spiritual and mystical.'

'And what's the difference?'

'The spiritual is towards your liberation. It is for the prisoner who is looking for a jail break. But when you have transcended the limitations of your physicality, you come into a different dimension altogether. You now encounter life in dimensions you haven't imagined possible. That's mystical. In Kailash both exist.'

'You know how to read all this knowledge off the face of a mountain,' I say after a pause. 'But what about the rest of us who are more or less illiterate?'

'Reading isn't just about literacy,' Sadhguru says with a smile. 'You don't try to read Kailash. When you are in a certain state of unfulfilment within yourself, you want to grasp. That won't work. You just learn to receive it. If you're not too full of yourself – not too full of the person that you made up, which is essentially a hallucination – receptivity happens.'

'And how do *you* receive Kailash?' I ask. I know I will have to find many ways of asking this question in the course of this trip. Sadhguru's responses are so tangential at times that I find myself reiterating the same question. It seems to be the best way to get as full and rich a reply as possible.

He doesn't answer. I repeat the question. He is silent for a long time. I wonder if he's forgotten and am debating whether to repeat it, when he suddenly says, 'When I see it, I go blind.'

'And that means…?'

'It means my visual apparatus doesn't function any more. When I ask you to close your eyes and meditate, that's what I am asking you to do. You're being asked to go blind.'

It reminds me of the line from Surdas, the blind bard of fifteenth-century India: 'For who has seen God but through eyes gone blind?'

I am thinking about the line when Sadhguru suddenly says, 'When Shiva came down from the highest possible experience, he danced. When he was in that highest experience, he just sat still.'

Like the mystic at the wheel, this land speaks the language of non sequitur, I think. Just when you grow accustomed to its grainy monochrome, a cobalt lake blazes into view. Or an emerald mountain, cloud-encrusted, or a flash of rhododendron. It vanishes as abruptly as it appears.

The image hangs in the air, as Tibet flashes past, a surreal blur of desert, ridge and abyss. I wonder, as I recurrently have, what exactly has brought me here. Several years ago, when I'd asked Sadhguru why the spiritual path seemed sometimes so solitary, bleak and devoid of reward, he'd offered a typically uncompromising reply. 'The seeker's only job is to stay one-pointed. When you decide to climb the mountain, you keep your gaze fixed on it. If there's a sunset on the way, you enjoy it. If there's a picnic on the way, you enjoy it. But you don't go looking for them. You stay one-pointed. Your focus is the mountain. You keep climbing.'

And I wonder if it's just my residual taste for literalism that has made me set out on this journey to what seems like the most challenging mountain of all. Thankfully, we aren't going to be attempting to climb it!

It is a journey I almost didn't make. Seized by an acute backache weeks before the trip, I wrote a secretly relieved mail to Sadhguru, informing him that I wouldn't be able to join the expedition. He wrote back a single line: 'Leave the troublesome topmost part of yourself behind and come.'

And so, four days later, with an orthopaedic belt around my waist, I found myself grimly standing in a queue to board a flight to Kathmandu, marvelling at my own insanity. Oddly, however, I have to concede, the pain began to subside soon after I boarded the flight. Now, it is niggling, but considerably diminished. I am too cautious to be relieved, anxious that I might be ambushed by it again at any time.

I return after a while to the theme of the mystical library. 'But why would Adiyogi download his knowing on a mountain? Is Kailash more receptive than other mountains?'

Sadhguru laughs. 'Mountains are not receptive. It's just that when a human being experiences something mystical – something beyond the limitations of the physical – rarely does he find an opportunity to share it with people around him. It's very difficult. Whatever you say, people will try to make a conclusion or philosophy out of it. I am doing my best to confuse you, but even now you are trying to unearth some philosophy!

'So most of it can never be shared, can never be spoken. It goes unexpressed. You know what you have is of phenomenal value but you cannot impart it for a variety of reasons. So you want to store it somewhere. The most efficient way to store knowledge is in the form of energy.

'When enlightened beings choose a mountain peak, it is because they are looking for a substance of a certain density. Otherwise, it won't work. When you want to store it in the form of energy, you need some kind of scaffolding.

'Mystics also choose a place that is difficult to reach, but not totally inaccessible. So Adiyogi would not have chosen Mount Everest, for instance, because it's too inaccessible. At the same time, he wouldn't choose some small hillock in southern India either, because every cowherd would walk on it.

'So, maybe in another hundred years, they will have a mountaintop resort here – a Kailash resort. You never know! There is an airport now a hundred kilometres from Kailash. So even a mountaintop resort – such a travesty – is possible...

'There are many mountains like this which have been chosen to store knowledge. But in sheer volume there is nothing comparable to Kailash. So it is not that Kailash is receptive. It is only holding things up. It is this mountain's fortune that Adiyogi chose it as a scaffold for his knowing.'

'And what about you?' I return to the subject of the self-proclaimed sidekick, my abiding source of interest. 'As a mystic, where do you download your knowing?'

Sadhguru smiles. 'There was a time when I was concerned about how to transmit what I knew. In my eagerness, I tried to prepare people to receive different dimensions. But in making these attempts, you can get into a lot of social and personal complications and misunderstandings. I have still not given up, but I'm much more relaxed now.

'Right from my infancy, my life was ruled by a mountain peak. That haunted me all my life till I found it. That was the Velliangiri Mountain – what we now call the Seventh Hill.

'But still I haven't stored what I know on a mountain. Instead, I created my own scaffolding: the Dhyanalinga. I'm at ease now mainly because I have had the fortune of being able to put everything that I am into that form.

'Some day, when somebody who is receptive enough comes there, he or she will know what it's about. I hope that day will come soon, but who knows when? Still, just knowing that it will be accessed some day has brought my life to a certain ease.

'If someone sits with absolute openness, they can access it all – everything that's worth knowing – right there in the comfort of the Dhyanalinga brick dome. I've repeatedly said that the stone form of the linga is not important; it is only a scaffold; you can even remove it. The real form is the energy form and that can never be destroyed.

'But if you find somebody that you can pour it into, that's great. I have been preparing people. We've done well. Compared to many others, we've done pretty well. Even Adiyogi had only seven, after all!'

I mull over the mechanics of mystical accession at Kailash. 'How is it done? How does one decide what to access? Is it catalogued in any way?'

There is uproarious laughter. 'You mean whether poetry is separated from fiction and history in this library? In a way, yes, it is catalogued. These dimensions are all traditionally seen as strands of Shiva's hair. You just pick up one strand and explore it.'

'What does Kailash mean to *you*?' I ask curiously. 'Why do you come to Kailash? How does it make you feel?'

Sadhguru laughs. 'Like a dud. With every layer that opens up there, I feel like an ignorant dud. I know enough to conduct this life for myself and for others. But Kailash reminds me that what I know is still very limited. If I sit there for a month or two, or maybe two years, it would just unfold endlessly. And it still wouldn't be exhausted.'

He chuckles. 'But then, in the world in which I operate I may become a crackpot! I'm sure you'll be one of the first people who will leave me because I'll start talking so unreasonably. So, every time I come, I read a book, a journal or, sometimes, just a chapter. Wanting to grasp the entire library will take more than a life.'

'But aren't you tempted to stay behind and download more?' I ask.

'It's not about temptation,' he replies. 'It is like going for a PhD, you understand? It is a certain investment of time you make to specialize. It is not useless; knowledge is never useless. Some day that knowing may open up a certain possibility. But if you are in pursuit of those things, it will occupy you full-time. In a lifetime there are only certain things you can choose to do. I've chosen to work with people. If I have to go on a total mysticism trip, I'll have to shut myself off from people completely. It will need undivided attention.'

'But surely you can –,' I begin.

He cuts in. 'Right now this air around you, you can study it for the rest of your life and learn its intricacies. You know nothing about that right now. But you breathe and you benefit from it. You know how to retain oxygen and let out carbon dioxide. You know how to use air, how to purify it, how not to pollute it. For now that's enough. For me that's enough.'

'You mean the impulse to grasp has fallen away,' I remark.

'If you choose to grasp, you do. Otherwise, you don't. Remember

Rishabha Maharishi? He went deeper and deeper into it. But at the end he didn't get Kailash; Kailash got him.

'I can just look at Kailash and be overwhelmed. Tears will come to me, but I can just bow down, and come back. I don't need to take everything it has.'

I think about my own urgent need to ply him with questions. It always feels like there will never be time enough to ask all that I have. There's probably a lesson in here for me somewhere.

The car comes to a halt on a ribbon of road. This is evidently the highest point on our trip.

As we get out of the car to stretch our legs, Sadhguru turns back to add, 'It's like trying to understand the ocean by drinking all of it. Just won't work.'

This has got to be the roof of the world, this chasm between geology and dream. I am beginning to understand the logic of this land – its frugality of form, its deceptive blankness. A mountain like Kailash, I imagine, would become a significant event in such spare choreography. It would compel you to pay attention. You couldn't miss it if you tried.

Around us are familiar Tibetan prayer flags, their bright reds and oranges the only blaze of colour in this chill landscape. 'Lha-so-so-so,' is the traditional Tibetan chant you're meant to intone every time you pass these flags. It means 'victory to the gods', I discover later. Sadhguru leads and we follow suit.

As soon as he gets out of the car, Sadhguru is swamped by the television crew behind us. While he does a quick television interview in Telugu, the rest of us wander around a desolate expanse of mountain, pebble, shrub and scree.

The winds blow unrelentingly. Before we know it, we are enveloped in a dense fusillade of cloud.

Half an hour later, we return to the car. Sadhguru seems upbeat. 'All the time in the world and a road to nowhere,' he says exuberantly, and starts intoning the 'Mahadevaya Namaha' chant.

I have heard him utter it many times before in his resonant voice at *satsangh*s. But wending our way now to the abode of Mahadeva himself, the chant seems different. The litany of Shiva's many names takes on another quality, strangely primal.

Mahadevaya Namaha
Yogishwaraya Mahadevaya
Tryambakaya Tripurantakaya
Trikagni Kalaya Kalagni Rudraya
Neelakanthaya Mrityunjaya…

Sadhguru's penchant for chanting is something that often confounded me in the past. On the one hand, he seemed like this no-nonsense yogi, rather than a purveyor of ritual and ceremony. And yet, he was often given to uttering Shiva-related chants from 'Brahmananda Swaroopa' to 'Shiva Shambho' and 'Mahadevaya Namaha'. What were they about? A token bow to cultural norms? A strategy to create an ambience of devotion? Or were these consecrated utterances? When he pauses, I insert the question.

'Just the sound "Shiva" is very powerful,' he answers. 'You don't have to believe anything; just the word can be explosive. In an advanced yoga programme, if seekers are sufficiently prepared, if I merely utter the word, they explode into a completely different level of energy and awareness. A mantra can be that powerful.'

'In the Adiyogi legend, Narada says that Adiyogi created himself out of his mastery over sound. What exactly does that mean?' I ask.

'We know through modern science also that every sound has a form attached to it and every form has a sound attached to it,' Sadhguru replies. 'This is a scientific fact. Through an oscilloscope you can know that every reverberation has a form. Today, science is also telling us that the whole of existence is just a vibration of energies. There is no such thing as matter any more, as far as science is concerned; the universe is just a web of reverberations. Where there is a vibration, there is bound to be a sound. Which means the whole of existence is just a complex web of sounds.

'Yoga has always said the whole of existence is sound. This is called *Nada Brahma* ("nada" means sound; "brahma" is creation). There is an ancient science of mantra, yantra and tantra based on this understanding. Mantra is pure sound. Yantra is its corresponding form. Tantra is the technology of using these two dimensions of mantra and yantra, sound and form, in a powerful way. This is a profound science. Nada Yoga is the science of using sound to become one with existence.'

I think of the Biblical line: 'In the beginning was the Word, and the Word was with God and the Word was God.'

'It's a truth expressed in some way or other across cultures,' Sadhguru responds. 'Lao Tzu speaks of the indefinable "unchanging Name". The Sufis say something similar: If the *anaam* (the nameless) had not wished to manifest and become *naam* (the name), there would be no sound and no creation.

'So, when Narada says Adiyogi is self-created, he means he is born of himself. His origin lies in that primordial sound that marks the beginning of existence. He has no parentage, no heritage, no past, no ancestry. When he has no past, it means he always belongs to the present. And considering the way the human intellect has evolved, he is definitely the solution for the future!

'He is born in the womb of silence. His pedigree is the first sound. He is the first manifestation of that reverberation – nada – which cannot be heard by the human ear, but can be experienced in deeper dimensions of perception. He is the most fundamental sound, the ultimate root of everything.'

Reluctant to interrupt, I realize I have grown more into listener than interlocutor. 'So how exactly does a mantra work?' I ask at length.

'There is a deep logic to it,' Sadhguru asserts. 'In the vast amalgamation of sounds in existence, a few key sounds have been identified as mantras. They are not religious, or sectarian; neither are they a form of worship. They are just keys to access the cosmic intelligence. Just like a key – a small piece of metal – a mantra is a small piece of sound, but if you know how to use it, it can open up a whole new dimension within the self.

'Generally, people invest emotion into the mantra that they make use of as they do not know the intensity of involvement without emotion. This is the reason why in this culture we brought method to devotion. A method essentially means a systematic process. Devotion is devoid of all process, but for the fruition of devotion, it is important that it does not turn hallucinatory, as overflowing emotions often do. Emotion can be a powerful way of making oneself vulnerable.'

'So, is the meaning of a mantra unimportant?' I ask. I know the enchantment of sound is more primary than its meaning. It is the logic of poetry.

'The mantra uses consecrated sounds as a passageway to existence. You just make it your life breath, so the sound is constantly on within you. If one moment of vulnerability comes, it will just crack you open. New things will happen, absolutely new things will happen.

'It is a pure science, but classical music in this land also developed beautiful and elaborate ways to access deeper dimensions. A large part of classical Indian music is pure mantra – no meaning, just a certain arrangement of sounds put together with mathematical precision. If one knows how to enter this complex arrangement, it can be a route towards the very basis of this existence. A mantra is mathematically perfect. Music, on the other hand, is mathematically correct, but more invested in the aesthetics of the sound.'

An invocation to Shambho – Shiva as a benevolent, personal god – is one that Sadhguru often uses. He has said that it has been his particular 'key'. It was an utterance evidently dear to someone very significant to him in another lifetime as well.

'My guru, Sri Palani Swami, lived on the mantra,' he says now. 'The priest of a local temple was hugely offended when he saw that this yogi was uttering the word all the time – even while attending to the calls of nature! The people around him tried to prosecute him for this offence and he was brought before the local panchayat for uttering the name of God inappropriately.

'He simply sat quietly before his jury, his eyes closed. And then, everyone around him clearly heard the sound "Shambho" emanating from his very body! They did not know what to make of that. They simply backed off.

'No one ever knew his name. His antecedents were unknown. Because he was seen in deep states of samadhi in the Palani Hills, he was referred to as Palani Swami.' Sadhguru laughs. 'For me, everything that I am comes from this simple sound. Everything I have done here in this lifetime springs from this simple utterance. It is my key to the beyond.'

The car falls silent. I watch the play of light over scarp and fissured mountain – grey, mauve, green, violet.

Minutes later, in a lighter vein, Sadhguru adds, 'A few years ago, someone came over from Australia and I happened to be with him in Mysore. I know the city so I am a good guide to have there. As I drive, I hear this person next to me saying "shit". If I drive a little fast, I hear "shit". If I brake, "shit". If the food is spicy, "shit". If the food is good, "shit". If we see something beautiful, "wow, shit". I kept wondering, what's the problem, is this person constipated?'

He laughs. 'But then I saw it was working for him. He is getting angry, he says "shit", and his anger settles down. Anything that is working for anybody, I don't want to disturb, you know? I am only interesting in dismantling things which are not working. With what is working, what is the problem? We say Shiva, he says shit! It's only a cultural difference.

'Even in the sound "Shiva", it is the "shi" which is powerful; "va" is more a damper, because people will go crazy otherwise with just "shi, shi, shi". So "va" is added to control that. So somehow half the world accidentally stumbled on this word "shit". It sounds somewhere about the same.'

There's much laughter over that one.

'Sacrilege,' I remark lightly.

'But am I equating shit with Shiva? I am not,' Sadhguru swoops in on my comment. 'Shiva is the highest and shit is shit. You cannot equate the two. But if you store things in your mind phonetically, you'll see these two sounds are bound to be next to each other.

'What is good and bad, what is sacred and filthy, once you divide this in your mind, your existence is divided. Once you divide existence there is no possibility of freedom, of transcendence for you.

'In yoga, either you see everything as divine or you see everything as filth. Both will work. There are two types of yogis. There are some yogis who see everything as divine. That's one way. Another kind sees everything as filth. The first thing in the morning, they get up and start their life with filthy words. Do you know this? This is common with the *aghoris* and some other groups. They curse everyone – their mothers, sisters, gurus, everybody, really. This is a whole mantra by itself. It takes a lot of creativity to come up with these cuss words! First thing in the morning, that's their worship!

'If you see everything as filthy, you will get through. If you see everything as sacred, you will get through. It's only when something is filthy and something else is sacred that you are stuck, because now you've divided the world. Yoga means union. Once you divide existence, you are finished.'

And this, I think, is quintessential Sadhguru: capable of offering a joke and an existential insight all in one breath. It reminds me just why he is my spiritual guide. The laughter and the learning are inseparable.

'To see everything as sacred, everything as divine, is an easier, more pleasant way to do it,' he continues. 'When I speak of "limitless responsibility" in every talk, this is what I mean. It means seeing *everything* as yours. Right now you think you are only responsible for one part of the world and not the other. That's the problem.

'The reality is that you are alive because your body and your energies are transacting with the rest of the cosmos all the time. Isn't that so? Only your mind has chosen to forget that. So, just choose to respond consciously and willingly to everything. Externally, of course, you react differently to situations and people according to your social situations. But, internally, it has to be the same intensity of involvement with all aspects. Only then there is a passage for you.

'Otherwise, once you divide existence, you have divided yourself. You are half a life. Half of you cannot get anywhere. You have to be a complete human being to go somewhere.

'If you want to do it the other way – if you want to see everything as filthy – you must withdraw and live somewhere else, not in social situations. Those on this path usually live alone. They will attain realization very quickly because it's a shortcut, but a very hard path.'

As I reflect on mantras as consecrated sound, I think back to an anecdote Sadhguru has related about his own childhood perception of sound as form. 'At school, most of the time, I simply stared at my teachers,' he said. 'As they talked, initially I understood the words. Then I suddenly realized that they were only making sounds, and I was making up the meanings in my head. So I stopped making up meanings. Suddenly, what was boring became very amusing. I was still staring, but with a big smile on my face. The teachers were not amused. I was giving them the kind of attention they'd never received in their lives! Initially, I heard the sounds, but after some time, I couldn't. I just started seeing all kinds of forms spewing out of their mouths, and I was just looking at them, wide-eyed.'

It was later in his life when he visited Kanti Sarovar – the legendary site of Adiyogi's historic exposition to the seven sages – that Sadhguru experienced something else: form as sound. I am aware that he had one of his most profound mystical experiences there. I try to steer the conversation in that direction.

'You've said that a Sanskrit chant descended upon you when you went to Kanti Sarovar many years ago, that you experienced the entire creation as sound.'

Sadhguru adjusts the rear-view mirror. His face looks suddenly taciturn, inscrutable.

The silence lengthens. I try to think of a new strategy to approach the subject when he suddenly says, 'If you are in a deep state of silence within, if you look at any form, the sound attached to that form will be clear to you. This is called *ritambhara pragna*. It means you just perceive forms as sounds. You are able to glean the reverberation of the form.

'It was more than twenty years ago when I first went to Kanti Sarovar. You know what it means? It is literally the "lake of grace". It is a little beyond Kedarnath in the Himalayas – a tricky climb. I set forth at around 2.00 or 2.30 p.m. It was a sunny day. It was warm. I think I got there in a little more than an hour. There was this incredible glacial lake and these snow-capped mountains all around.

'I climbed up and sat on one of the rocks. In terms of natural beauty, it was fantastic. The lake was huge. It was yet to become ice at that time. It was absolutely still water. No vegetation. Just snow-covered peaks reflected in totally still water. An incredible view. What happened to me after that is very difficult to describe.

'Basically, everything just turned into sound – the mountain, the lake, my own body. It was all just sound and it was reverberating inside me in a completely different way. I had suddenly slipped into a state of ritambhara pragna.

'Now, I have had a deep appreciation for Sanskrit as a language, and I've had opportunities to learn it. But I have always avoided it because the moment you learn Sanskrit, you will invariably end up reading the scriptures. I didn't want to do that. My own vision has never failed me, and I didn't want to clutter myself with all these traditions.

'But now, here I was, my eyes open, my mouth closed – I am very clear about that – but my own voice was going on loudly, as if it was on a microphone, singing a song in Sanskrit. I heard it clearly, loudly, in *my* voice. So loud, it was like the whole mountain was singing. I thought this lasted for maybe ten or fifteen minutes, but when I came back to my normal senses, the sun had set and it was about 6.30.

'I didn't compose this. It just descended upon me. If you just give yourself to that song, it has the power to dissolve you:

Nada Brahma Vishwaswaroopa
Nada hi Sakala Jeeva Roopa
Nada hi karma, Nada hi dharma
Nada hi bandhana, Nada hi mukti
Nada hi Shankara, Nada hi Shakti
Nada Brahma Vishwaswaroopa
Nadam Nadam, Sarvam Nadam
Nadam Nadam, Nadam Nadam

(Sound is Brahman, the manifestation of the universe, sound manifests itself in the form of all life, sound is bondage, sound is the means of liberation, sound is that which binds, sound is that which liberates, sound is the bestower of all, sound is the power behind everything, sound is everything.)

'That's when I realized that Sanskrit is a language created in a particular way – it is based on the awareness of the root sound connected to every form. When you utter that sound, you also have access to that form; if you master the sound, you have mastery over the form. The language is the consequence of ritambhara pragna, not a language created for the sake of communication alone. In Sanskrit, the utterance of the sound is more important than the meaning. Most languages are created for meaning, for the sake of communication. But here, simply uttering the sounds creates a certain situation within you. It is like the blueprint of existence.'

'Is that a means that Adiyogi used with his seven sages?' I ask. 'Nada Yoga? Is that what he taught?'

Sadhguru laughs. 'Sound is still a physical entity. It is the subtlest form of physicality. Using sound is a good preparation for transcendence. It can create the right ambience. But the spiritual opens up only when you transcend from sound to silence.'

'So how did he teach?'

'When Adiyogi transmitted the science of yoga to the seven sages, he rarely spoke. He taught them all kinds of intricate and complex things, but not all of it was in words. Often he simply sat before them, intoxicated, his eyeballs rolled up. They sat there, the seven of them, receiving seven different dimensions of yoga. This happened for many years. He simply sat there, totally uninterested in those people.'

'But he did talk to Parvati,' I counter.

'To her, he spoke in loving ways. In incredibly tender ways.'

'Because she needed language?'

Sadhguru responds with a story. 'There was a great Zen master. He ran a monastery with over a thousand monks. One day, the townspeople heard the chanting of sutras, sacred texts. That is when they knew the master was no more.'

Conversations with a mystic, I realize, are emphatically not Chinese roads. You never know where you'll end up – you could start out on a train to Coimbatore and end up in a Land Cruiser in Tibet. I decide to think about that reply later.

The conversation turns to other subjects. I daydream, tuning in and out of the conversation. After a while, I wake from a fitful snooze to find a perfectly conical, inverted mountain outside my window. Is this what it means to be in the highest country on the planet? Have I really reached the roof of the world in some terrifyingly literal sense? A moment later, I realize I am simply looking at one of those opaline lakes that Tibet abounds in. Reflection in this land can be more heightened than reality.

It is almost half an hour later when Sadhguru returns, just as suddenly, to where we left off.

'When the real thing is gone, priests will fill a place; rituals will fill a place; mantras will fill a place,' he says. 'But these can never be a replacement for the fundamental spiritual process. Mantras have their beauty, no doubt about it, but no mantra is comparable to silence. No external method can compare with that fundamental source of creation throbbing within your very being. You turn to mantras if you don't know how to access that. When a master is present, that is never necessary.'

'So Parvati needed words, and the sages didn't?' I ask again.

'When Parvati saw Adiyogi sitting in silence, she asked him, "These great sages are sitting here before you. Why don't you say something to them?"

'He said, "Oh, they hear me."

'What he was actually telling her was: "Because of your intimacy with me, invested in emotion, you don't hear me, so I have to speak to you. *They* hear me."

'The yogic tradition has spoken of different dimensions of sound. There is the physical dimension – the sound which can be spoken and heard. There is the intermediary dimension – the vibration of thought, which is the word or sound produced by the mind. There is the third dimension, which is the mind's ability to create and produce sound from some deep recess, without any external input or stimulus. The fourth dimension is *para vak.* "Vak" means voice; "para" means the divine or the source of creation. It means the voice of the Creator. It is the sound of the utterly still, soundless consciousness.

'Today, every scatterbrain in the world has been hearing God speak. A few years ago, he even spoke in the White House! I am not talking about those who concoct or imagine according to their convenience. Not that kind of "God spoke to me" nonsense. I am talking about the reverberation that is the basis of everything. Unless you hear *anaadhi*, the beginning-less sound – that which is the basis not only of creation but the Creator also – you will not know fulfilment.

'If you try to learn about the different aspects of creation, it will be an endless journey, because it is an endless universe. But if you hear the beginning-less sound, it is all right here. You don't have to extend yourself into an endless process of learning.'

We are quiet. 'And how does one hear the beginning-less sound?' I ask after a pause.

'Right now, the *only* two instruments that you have to know anything about are your body and your mind. If we have to make these into instruments which hear the very basis of the cosmic consciousness, they have to be in a certain state of purity. This means you have *become* the life process. Only life can perceive life and its source.

'If you have to perceive the subtler and deeper dimensions of life, you have to be alive in the highest possible way. The whole process of yoga is to turn body, mind and energy into instruments of perception that enable you to perceive the beginning-less. Both the creation and the Creator have a beginning. But anaadhi is that without beginning or end, that which cannot be seen, held, conquered or captured – it can only be heard. Once you hear that, you are utterly, absolutely fulfilled.

'That is what Shiva meant when he said, "They hear me." He did not mean, "They hear what is happening in my mind." He meant, "They hear the basis of my consciousness, and that's all they need to hear."'

Western Tibet rolls by outside my window – rugged, primal, strangely dreamlike. And, suddenly, all this talk seems less far-fetched, less incongruous. It feels like this is the right conversation for this particular landscape. This is the kind of place where one might see a yogi, a snake around his neck, a crescent moon in his matted locks, his body a vivid, compelling blue... And it wouldn't seem out of place.

But there is also a part of me that is vaguely restless. It takes me time to lay my finger on my unease.

And then I understand. When Sadhguru talks of Shiva, he's talking about someone very real to him. I can see it in the way his face lights up. I hear it in the animation in his voice, the exuberance in his song. Shiva is as real for him as I am – and a thousand times more precious.

But for me, none of this makes much sense. The stories are interesting, it is true, but eventually, they're stories. In short, they're spiritual gossip. I don't know Shiva. Yes, I grew up with tales of him. I found them awe-inspiring, unsettling. But that apart, I don't have a personal equation with him. He's not my personal god. He's not the subject of my mantra. He's not a concept I really understand. On some very basic level, I feel excluded.

Sadhguru is on his way to meet his partner in crime, his accomplice, his beloved, his life breath. And I? I'm on my way to a mountain.

Sadhguru catches my eye in the rear-view mirror. I know he's read my thoughts.

'It doesn't matter how you see him,' he says. 'There is always something more to him.'

'And is there room for sceptics here?' I ask, wondering if my journey has any meaning at all.

'There is no better sceptic than the spiritual seeker,' says Sadhguru. 'The spiritual process is just scepticism formalized. For a seeker, personal emancipation is the most important thing. Nothing else matters. That makes the seeker a sceptic in the best sense of the term.

'Unfortunately, suspicion is mistaken for scepticism. For a suspicious person, the spiritual experience is completely out of his reach. But not for the sceptic. The sceptic has doubts. That's fine. Doubt is healthy. But suspicion is different. Suspicion is a sickness.'

'And even if I approach Shiva as a devotee –,' I begin.

'You still don't know anything about it. Devotion is not an effort to grasp. It is the wild abandon of dissolution. The same "Mahadevaya namaha" could be uttered with so many dimensions of depth and understanding. There's no end to it.'

I am silent.

Sadhguru says, suddenly gentle. 'Think of it like this. Think of the day you came to your first programme in the ashram. The word "Sadhguru" – does it mean something different to you today?'

I know the answer to that one. I couldn't even bring myself to use the word for a long time. It seemed too alien, too hierarchical, too presumptuous. Why should I call this person my guru? Was he my guru at all? I avoided addressing him as much as I could.

Then, suddenly, the word is part of my life. The word now is not just a person – it is a presence. It is linked to the man at the wheel in front of me, but it is bigger than him too.

'It's just like that,' Sadhguru cuts into my thoughts. 'In a much, much bigger dimension, understanding Shiva is just like that.'

Our Toyota thunders on into the howling wilderness of the Tibetan plateau.

FACE-TO-FACE WITH THE AXIS OF THE WORLD

A mountain is a mountain. Or so I've always believed. Despite all that Sadhguru says about scaffolds and knowledge repositories, a mountain is still a mountain, as far as I can see.

It is true, some are endowed with more height, more girth, more grandeur. But in this pageant spread-out before us, Kailash isn't short on competition.

Still, there is the obvious difference. Even with the sinister blanket of cloud that hangs heavily across our landscape this morning, it is evident that this mountain allows itself some distinction. Amid these mountains of snow-lathered green and garnet, this is the only granite mountain we can see. Dark, forbidding, cloud-smothered, it stands implacably, a postcard pinned to our grimy window, a reminder of why we are here.

Meru, Shambhala, sky pillar, Shiva linga – I don't know about any of that, but the view at my window is proof that Kailash exists. Or, perhaps, it is just that we have entered the postcard ourselves. That seems equally possible. Breathing this rarefied air, it is possible we have stumbled into a subtler dimension and are now postcard pilgrims about to participate in a collective optical illusion, about to discover that the divide between fact and fiction has always been obscure, cloudy, snow-congealed.

The Tibetans believe, I am told, that this still point in a turning world is actually a visitor, an alien – a flying mountain that had to be tethered to the earth by the gods and finally secured by the Buddha's four decisive footprints. It is a reluctant visitor too. In Kaliyuga, the age of degeneration, it yearns to be elsewhere and is likely to take wing at any time. For all its solidity, that is also easy to believe. One day, the denizens of this hotel could well wake up to find their windows turned into empty slates, wiped clean of aeons of visual habit.

And it is for this that we made this trip, I reflect as I stand on our first-floor landing before breakfast. It is for this black convulsion of earth with its endless train of legend, its reputation stretching across millennia, way back into ancestral memory.

Is it worth the journey?

I decide to suspend judgement. I might not be able to take the burden of anticlimax right now. I don't have the breath for it.

All I know over breakfast is this: I am colder than I have ever been. I cannot eat a bite. I am down to tea and periodic infusions of hot water and honey. The slightest exertion makes me aware of my lungs like never before. The bathrooms are unspeakable. The yard in front of the hotel is a picturesque riot of yak shit. The rain is incessant. Everyone around me looks the way I feel – bewildered, battered, in varying states of medical disrepair. Two members of our group have been on oxygen all night. Conversation is sporadic. The Sounds of Isha music team is rehearsing, trying feebly, if valiantly, to infuse some fervour into the dining room (the one which doubles up as a dormitory and pantry and smells like it, I think uncharitably). It's difficult to ignore the wheezing breaths and occasional nosebleeds.

And yet, oddly enough, we are whole. Smiles are wan but they haven't disappeared yet. If I could sit motionless through the day, nursing a mug of tea, I tell myself, it's possible that I'll survive.

My breath is reasonably even when I sit still. The cold could be manageable if I don't leave this space. (There are advantages of having a versatile single room; never unused, it carries the residual warmth of continued human habitation.)

It is at 1 p.m. that we get the news. Sadhguru has announced that he is making a trek uphill towards Kailash. Those of us who are inclined can join him. The clouds have cleared. 'The sun,' a volunteer pops her head in to announce with admirable cheeriness, 'is out. Kailash is visible. Come on!'

An uphill trek when climbing to my first-floor room feels like an expedition to the stars? I stare at my shoelaces and slowly shake my head. Each time it feels like the demands can't get more outrageous, they do.

And so, of course, I spend the next hour and a half following Sadhguru up the mountain.

It is at this point that I probably should abandon understatement. It is time to let go of the last vestige of self-respect. To claim to be witness-archivist any more would be a sham.

I may have started out on this trip as a seeker-observer. A sympathetic one, it is true. Committed to my guru, it is true. But still, if I were honest, I have been oscillating for the large part of this week between respectful observer and cautious participant.

At some point the day before, however, I'd realized the extent to which the journey had diminished me. I had been pared down to a pilgrim. Nothing more and nothing less. Footsore, travel-weary, breath-rationed, bewildered, like everyone else around me. Helpless, ineffectual, leaning on wooden staffs and sturdy Sherpas, the stoic strength of yaks and the goodwill of fellow-travellers for support.

But, at this point, I have been whittled down even further. There isn't much of a choice about it either. If I were to look at the path winding endlessly before me, it wouldn't take much time before I sink down and accept defeat.

The only strategy, I discover, is one step at a time. And one breath – one shuddering breath – at a time.

But, of course, the mind that is wily enough to think up strategies is also wily enough to see through them. And so it ought to be a matter of minutes before I give in to the inevitability of failure and beat a retreat.

The fact is I don't.

I admit that this has nothing to do with tenacity or courage. After a dip I managed in Lake Manasarovar, I carried a soupçon of pride, perhaps not entirely unpardonable. Pride at my capacity for endurance, for being game enough to brave the elements, for midlife recklessness. But, at this point, I know that not a single step I take has anything to do with me.

Which brings me to my confession: I am now, quite simply, whether I like it or not, a devotee. The only way I make this ascent – past a twisting, winding panorama of stream and crag, past tidal waves of rock surging upward and sky nose-diving into cloud-slathered valley – is by pinning my gaze on the guru. It is the sight of his form ahead of me, sure of foot, long of stride, nimbly negotiating the path ahead, that keeps me going. Each time it feels like agony to put the next foot forward, each time it feels like my lungs are going to burst, I focus on him. In savage terror, in desperate trust. If he is my guru, he has to ensure I make it. I don't have much mind left now, or much body, or very much breath. If he is my guru, he has to carry me along.

And I find that although the prospect of a trek is still hair-raising, I am able somehow to take the next step. The next breath. And then the next.

Periodically, he turns. His gaze sweeps over us all, alert, calm, dispassionate. On a couple of occasions it rests on me. I realize then that he knows the truth as well as I do – the fact that I am, in fact, subsisting on his presence. Perhaps others are too.

It feels like an era before we halt. In actuality, it has taken us just a little over an hour. Sadhguru decides that we should stop by a waterfall. As I take my last few steps, faltering and stumbling, he looks down at me, his gaze not unkind.

'You're doing well,' he says quietly.

It takes me time to reply. 'Because of you,' I say inarticulately, short on breath.

His eyes glimmer with amusement. He is not unaccustomed to my long-standing distaste for overstatement. This clearly doesn't sound like me. It is now, however, a fact, a bald statement of truth.

I manage to add, 'And my back. The pain. It's gone.'

'So miracles do happen,' he says lightly. He has turned away before I can respond.

I subside on a rock. We are now at the highest point of our climb – over 17,500 feet. When I look down, I marvel at how far we have climbed. The hotel now seems like a distant speck below us. Looking at the path we have taken uphill, it feels like we have travelled more than a couple of kilometres. But it is not the hotel or the path behind us that commands our attention after a moment. It is what lies before us: this towering presence, striated by snow, swathed in endless diaphanous tissues of mist. Black, enormous, emphatically present.

If the invariable human problem with the sacred is its intangibility, its elusiveness, here all complaints are surely laid to rest. For here is reality in capital letters. Here is mountain – solid, physical, eminently tactile. And here is metaphor – richly veined, textured, inflected by aeons of spiritual folklore. The result of this conjunction between the physical and the metaphysical, between the literal and the emblematic is Shiva frozen eternally in form. Or, to put it another way, here is simply the staggering sight of centuries of abstraction – of incredible mythological and mystical sophistication – embodied in unequivocal stone. Here is idea made image. The conceptual made concrete. Thought turned thingy. Miracle as mountain.

No pilgrim, no aesthete – no one, I decide – could ask for more.

For the next hour, twenty of us sit meditating on the mountain. The chant of 'Tryambakaya Mahadevaya' accompanies us.

Later, I ask others in the group what this experience meant to them. 'Magic,' says S. 'The deepest meditation I've ever had,' says A. 'Time stood still,' says T. 'It was my seventh time,' says M, 'and it still took my breath away.' 'Bliss,' says K. Swami N merely smiles. Our young 'non-meditator' photographer from Delhi grins. 'I was busy shooting Sadhguru and all of you in your meditative trances and explosive states,' he says mischievously. 'But then I started shooting Kailash. And the closer I went to the mountain, something began to happen…' he pauses. 'Man, that mountain's alive.'

In my case, I'm not sure what exactly that hour meant. But with Sadhguru seated a few feet behind and the mountain in front, I do remember being aware that this was the defining moment of my journey, the point of my pilgrimage – a pilgrimage that began much earlier than ten days ago. This is the hour I will look back on, I told myself, the hour I will remember, the hour that I will wonder at for the rest of my life. This is the stuff of personal myth, the point at which a bunch of seemingly random human histories – mine and the rest of the group's – intersect with the beyond without any of us ever being any wiser of what that intersection really means.

The mountain begins to pulsate. Perhaps it is the effect of moving cloud and shifting light. The effect of being in a place that swims between fact and symbol. Or, perhaps, it's just the altitude. Or the Diamox I'm dosing on to counter it. Or, perhaps, it's the two accomplices at work yet again: the master and his 'fifty per cent partner'. I wonder if they even know, as partners in crime, where one's sphere of influence ends and the other's begins.

Then the tears start. And great wracking sobs. And so prose ends and another language takes over.

'WHEN YOU ARE IN
DESPERATE NEED'

The energy of ascent is different from the energy of descent. The pilgrimage to a sacred site is always distinct from the return home.

There is an imperceptible relaxing, a letting down of guard. I can allow myself to throw away my Diamox strips, to feel fatigue, allow my limbs to ache, let my appetite return. And as older rhythms start reasserting themselves, a familiar churning returns.

As I sit in the hotel lobby at Saga after breakfast looking out at a landscape of haggard, snow-doused greyness, breathing in air that suddenly seems thicker, less bracing, I think about the mountain that is Shiva's abode. Been there, done that, says the spiritual imperialist within me, bustling and self-important.

Has it changed me in any enduring way? Altered my self-perception? Transformed my understanding of the world?

I am a weathered enough pilgrim to know that the deepest changes are the subtlest. So I'm aware that the real impact of this journey, if any, won't be discernible until much later. It will creep up when I least expect it. So I'm not terribly perturbed by the small inner voice that asks the question: 'Yes, but what did it mean, *really*?'

I find myself thinking of Kartikeya and the fruit – a story that has always struck me as unfair. Why couldn't Adiyogi and Parvati have laid down the rules more clearly? Why couldn't they have said that it was a trick question? That it wasn't meant to be taken literally? That every journey is essentially an interior one?

But would Kartikeya have been ready to hear that before he left? Or, was he too consumed by wanderlust, by a raging thirst to explore the external world? Perhaps that race needed to be run anyway – until the rest of him caught up with that received wisdom?

I think of other undocumented travellers, those who undertake courageous, unmapped journeys. I think of the many prostrate, rolling figures wrapped in rough blankets we have seen on the way to Kailash, turning slowly, doggedly along the path, committed to a painstaking bodily circumambulation of the mountain.

What about those of us who are committed to a spiritual path but still feel the need to linger at some campfires, take a few detours, wander down a few alleyways? What about those of us who trudge along tamer yak trails, making a less heroic journey around the world? Those of us who clutch at our freight of personal stories and frayed dreams, inclined to play protagonist in our life dramas for just a little while longer?

Will the fruit keep? Will the mountain wait? Is there hope for the laggardly, the dreaming, the distracted, the forgetful? And will it continue to remain somewhere in our peripheral line of vision – that black summit, now earth, now emblem, swathed in a great white hush of Himalayan cloud?

My mind races now. I'm not looking at this experience for meaning; that seems too crassly utilitarian. I know that my quest thus far has not really been for the meaning of life, as much as a more intense, heightened experience of life itself. That Kailash has given me, undeniably.

But I still do want to know how it all connects.

At the heart of it is my lingering disquiet about Shiva as 'that which is not'. What does that 'vast emptiness' mean? What does the limitless blackness entail? Is it a universe denuded of all meaning?

Will I ever be ready for that?

I understand increasingly the role of the pause in poetry. I understand the role of silences in conversation. I feel the need for more blank spaces in my life than ever before. But a pause without a terminus? A silence without end? An interminable blankness? Is that what it's about? And if so, will I ever be ready for Adiyogi?

I think of Adiyogi's remark that the universe can be contained in a mustard seed. It reminds me of Blake's line about 'the universe in a grain of sand and eternity in an hour'. And I wonder about the connection between the concrete, the singular, the intimate, on the one hand, and the great cabbage soup of universality, on the other.

How does 'that which is not' connect with a passionate lover, a cosmic dancer, a compassionate guru? Why does the formless assume shape, size, texture, preference – the whole kit and caboodle of selfhood? Why does the impersonal turn personal? Why does the universal turn particular? Why does the supremely self-contained, autonomous Shiva succumb to Shakti's dance of otherness, if all it means is separation, fragmentation, disunity? If all it means are cycles, patterns, the rigmarole of birth and decay? Surely, he knows better?

I relate to myth. Over the years, I've grown to value it more than the language of metaphysics. I revel in its non-linear leaps, its twists, its slippages. But I cannot find a point of entry here. Something stays unsatisfying. Something remains untold.

The questions are not merely cerebral. For at the heart of all this churning is my guru. The man who embodies this mystery more than any other human being I know – the mystery of yogic dispassion with a vibrant humanness, an inwardness and composure with an understanding of the deep technology of the heart.

It was this mystery that drew me to Sadhguru all those years ago. It is this mystery that I am still trying to understand. Not logically. I know that being in his presence tells me more than trying to figure him out.

But old habits die hard. And besides, I know he enjoys a sparring session on occasion as much as I do.

I plunge into the deep end.

'So, what does it all mean?' I say half an hour into our car journey from Saga to Kathmandu. 'What does Adiyogi mean really? What do his stillness and his action mean? What makes him engage in either?'

Sadhguru responds with a story he's told before. 'When Adiyogi told the seven sages to go out into the world and spread his yoga, they were apprehensive. What if the world did not understand it? Would they be successful? So Adiyogi told them: "When you are successful, I will help you. When you are in desperate need, I will sleep."'

I'm not sure I have ever made my peace with that one. 'Why would he go to *sleep?*'

'You don't like it.' He laughs.

I can't say I do.

'It means he is that much more effective when he is not moving, not in action.'

He spends the next five minutes fiddling with his music system, adjusting his rear-view mirror and asking a volunteer to ferret out a snack. I decide to focus on a splintered skyline through mountain and ravine, assuming he's forgotten the conversation, when he suddenly remarks, 'And that's the way I am. I keep blabbing because that's what the world understands. But I'm much more effective when I'm sitting with my eyes closed.'

'But what makes inaction more effective?'

'What Adiyogi is saying is, "If you cannot see, I'll turn off the lights."'

'How does that help?'

'It is the highest level of help! But the logical mind won't like it. It is only when the lights are off that you see where the flaw lies, where the problem is. If you don't see the flaw, you cannot fix it. That's meditation – to find the flaw, to see the blind spot. Once you've seen it, there's no problem any more. If the spot was on the floor, you would have found it. But it's in the eyeball, that's the problem. So you have to close your eyes and sit – and then you know what you need to know.

'That's what I did. Wanting to know life, I stared till my eyeballs popped at just about everything. The more attention I paid, the more complex it got. It is only when I closed my eyes for long periods of time that the universe yielded and blossomed within me.

'What Adiyogi is offering you is the ultimate possibility. If you can see in the dark, why would you feel the need for light at all?'

It is a reply that gives me pause. I know it will take time to internalize. For now, time is short and I try approaching it another way. 'Why do you take these hundreds of people to Kailash year after year when it makes so much more sense for you to go alone? What's the motivation?'

'It doesn't make sense for you to be here?' he asks lightly.

It does. But the question remains.

'Because if you don't engage, people will remain lost in their stupid problems,' he says. 'They are capable of creating a problem for every solution. They will never think of liberation.'

'Can "liberation" mean an escape from this world?' I ask. 'It sometimes seems that way.'

'Why would it be an escape when we're talking about engaging with the world?'

'How do you reconcile this with Shiva going to sleep when he's needed most?'

'I told you, he's the silent partner,' Sadhguru is still laughing. 'I'm the active one. All the slog is mine.'

'So why are you slogging?' I persist.

'It doesn't feel like slogging. It's just that when you take up some work, you want to do it as best as you can. The day I decide it's off, it will be off.'

'And does love come into this somewhere?'

Sadhguru seizes on that. 'So you think love is the ultimate.'

I admit that it is pretty significant. I can't conceive of life without it.

'Why do you want love? Because it gives you moments of bliss. But if you could have a method by which you could be blissful always, why would you want love? Love is a pleasant way to be; that's fine. But most people are trying to fulfil a certain sense of incompleteness by trapping someone in some emotion.'

'Compassion then?'

'Why would you want compassion? Recently at a programme, I asked the participants, "What kind of world do you want to live in?"'

'A young girl stood up and said, "A compassionate world."'

'I said, "See, you're still young. But one day, when you get married, do you want a husband who's passionate or compassionate?"'

'Immediately, she said, "Passionate!"'

'She wants passion, but with the rest of the world, she wants to dispense compassion! What is that? Magnanimous!

'As far as I'm concerned, I'm indiscriminately passionate about anything and everything I come in touch with. Do you want someone to be kind and compassionate to you? Or, do you want someone who is passionately engaged with life on all levels?

'We have unfortunately segregated these words so that "passion" for most people means something physical or sexual, and "compassion" means a saintly way of doing things. It is not so. Passion means unbridled involvement. And involvement is

the only way to know the taste of life. A selective involvement can
become entangling. But an indiscriminate involvement becomes
your liberation.'

It feels like we're digressing. 'Why would you engage with the
world if there was no love or compassion? In larger terms, why does
Shiva get involved? Isn't love the motivation? That's my question.'

Sadhguru lifts up his hands in exasperation. 'I've repeated this
in so many ways. The word "yoga" means union. The yogi cannot
distinguish most of the time between what he is, what the car is,
what the road is. He cannot distinguish between himself and the
rest of the world. Because there's no car, there's no road, there's no
world, there's no him. Okay?'

I've heard this before. But I want to hear it again. I want the
insider's account. Each time I hear it, it gives me a surge of wonder.
It awes me to think I am sitting next to a person who inhabits his
inner space in such a vastly different way.

He continues. 'If you throw the boundary of your sensation out in
an expanded form, you can sit right here and experience everything
and everyone, the very cosmos, as your body. This is not some moral
value. This is how a human being is *made*. Right now if your little
finger is damaged, do you need a god-given mandate to fix it? Or,
is it natural to want to fix it?'

'Natural,' I begin.

'That's all there is to it,' he says definitively.

I understand – at least theoretically. Sadhguru is seldom
reassuring. But to be a little finger in the hand of a true lama (as the
Tibetans call him), I decide for now, is not to be scoffed at.

The classical theatre of the land unfolds at my window – wild,
calcified, purified of excess, bleached of sentiment.

A long time later, I try to find a way into my next question. It will not be easy. But I still need to ask it. It is the same greed to hear from a living insider what the enlightened condition is about.

I am long accustomed to Sadhguru's strategies of evasion. All my attempts to get him to describe the state of self-realization have met with cryptic replies. I know he is in a long lineage of masters who have refused to falsify or distort the ultimate by rendering it in the language of duality. The Buddha is, of course, a glorious example of that brand of uncompromising silence. And yet, even he came close to an admission: 'If there were not a not-made, not-compounded, not-born, there would not be a made, a compounded, a born.'

Sadhguru's descriptions thus far have all been equally elliptical. 'Wild emptiness,' was the most evocative one I've heard from him so far. But some part of me wants something more inviting. I understand Sadhguru's resistance to mystical romanticism, but I want to see if I can get him to speak of the sacred in less negative terms.

I decide to play contrarian. I return to the image of the hand and the fixing of fingers. 'So even if it is not love that motivates the yogi to engage with the world, what's the point of the whole journey from emptiness to form to emptiness? Why?'

'If you ask me why,' says Sadhguru with a twinkle, 'I can give you a story, and you have the choice to believe it or not. I'm not here to tell you why. I'm here to show you how, how to be free of those cycles. That is yoga.'

And so, we are back to the start of Adiyogi's exposition to the seven sages. But I don't want to abandon this line of questioning just yet. 'Why would we as seekers yearn for emptiness? Why would we yearn for Shiva if he spells oblivion?'

Sadhguru shakes his head. 'What you're doing right now is trying to make diamond jewellery with a pickaxe; you will not make jewellery like that. Jewellery needs fine instruments.'

'And only the mystic has those implements?'

'Everyone can have them. Everybody has them. They've forgotten. They're too happy with their pickaxe, hacking at everything with their intellect.'

I persist. 'Often,' I say, 'it sounds like one must do years of spiritual penance just to reach the realization that nothing matters.'

'This is what so many philosophers have concluded,' says Sadhguru, 'because they never looked at life experientially.'

'I'm asking you as someone who's looked at it experientially,' I tell him. 'You say there is no connection between the psychological and the existential, and that bothers me.'

'Is it true that the five people in this car can have five different types of psychological drama going on?'

I nod.

'The reality is that five people are travelling in a car at a hundred and thirty kilometres an hour. But the drama that's going on in your head need not have anything to do with the reality. So you agree that these dramas have nothing to do with the existential? That they are make-believe?'

'Self-created, perhaps,' I agree. 'And not entirely miserable.'

'But it's still make-believe, isn't it? Now do you see that for most people, the self-created drama or the psychological condition is turning against them? It is often a source of misery.'

'But waking up from the make-believe to realize that reality is just limitless emptiness is not a very encouraging prospect,' I point out.

Sadhguru is impatient. 'You're not going step by step. You've already jumped ahead and concluded that life is meaningless.'

I subside into silence.

'Take it a step at a time. Now your psychological condition needs treatment if it's turning against you, doesn't it? So though every experience is largely self-created, human beings are largely creating unpleasantness for themselves.

'Right now, I'm telling you it's a complete life, but you have not realized how complete it is. You're living on the surface and you've decided it's incomplete. So you start a whole circus and try to glorify and sanctify that circus. All because you're unwilling to make the necessary effort to go deeper into yourself.'

'But going deeper seems to entail reaching a point where nothing seems to matter,' I say.

'That's because you're standing on this side and making conclusions about the other side without knowing what it is. I have you read *Flatland*? It's a nineteeth-century novella about two-dimensional beings landing up in a three-dimensional world, and the conclusions they make.'

'You've said before that the experience of enlightenment is like an endless free fall through an abyss, and that sounds alarming,' I add.

'The terror is only about hitting the bottom, not about falling. If the consequence is taken away, what's the problem? Ever tried skydiving?'

I shudder. 'Sometimes it sounds like spirituality is only for those with a taste for adventure sports,' I remark.

'Not true. How did you come to that conclusion?'

'When you talk of breaking limitations, or free-falling endlessly through darkness, there's nothing gentle or comforting about it.'

He laughs heartily. 'What's terrifying about it? And anyway, life is like that. What's wrong with it? Creation started with a bang. The scientists told you that. I didn't. You want it to start with a tinkle? And what do you do with eggs? You want eggs to flower into an omelette? No, you have to break them.'

'Gentler metaphors would help,' I suggest.

'It's very important that the words used are negative, otherwise people could turn fanciful and hallucinatory. Spirituality and fancifulness are very close. So always negative terminology – shoonya, nirvana – was used to guard against that.

'If you think the body is all you have, the prospect of losing it is terrifying. There are people who will fight to death for five rupees, because that's all they have. But if someone comes and fights with you for five rupees, you'll just give it away. Why? Because you have a bank balance. It's the same for the yogi. There is no more fear because you know you are not your body or your mind; you are in constant touch with the truth. You have your bank balance. You are one with life.'

'But what is that bank balance in existential terms? You say that the ultimate face of Shiva is utter darkness, no-thingness.' I know I am pushing the point, but I want him to say more.

'Trying to grasp the existential through the psychological won't help,' says Sadhguru dismissively. 'Through the make-believe you're trying to grasp reality – it will never work like that.'

He pauses. 'This speck of human life is so insignificant, and still the very source of creation is active in it. The Creator still finds it worthwhile to be active in this speck. That means there must be something else other than the speck, isn't it?'

We have arrived at the admission of 'something else'.

I realize that this is as far as we're likely to get. It is still mysterious, but a tad more reassuring. I feel mildly vindicated.

'And that something else cannot be talked about –,' I say cautiously.

'But it can be experienced,' says Sadhguru. 'If we talk about it, wrong conclusions will be drawn. Like you've concluded that if it is empty it must be meaningless. And then people live their lives with those conclusions and make philosophies out of them.'

He laughs. 'Unfortunately, when you perceive reality the way it is, you get labelled a mystic. You should actually be labelled a normal human being.'

I am back to my favourite subject: the inner experience of the mystic at the wheel. 'So as the only "normal" human being in this car, what do you perceive at this very moment? Are you experiencing reality the way it is right now?'

'If I experience everything as it is, I won't be able to drive. When I need to, I know how to put my hallucination on. And right now,' Sadhguru chuckles, his foot hard on the accelerator, 'I am also sharing the Chinese hallucination of a concrete road!'

I watch mountain and ridge unfurl and contract – a perfect martial art of geography. I know it is time for this exchange to wind down. The journey is approaching its close. We should be driving into Nepal soon. I return to the story of the primordial mystic.

'What happened to Adiyogi? How did his story end? Did he die?'

'No, he did not die.'

'He went back? He dematerialized?'

'He went back, maybe. He dismantled himself, put back what he had gathered here from the earth and went back. There is no grave site for him. No story in the lore ever talks about his death. That's because no such thing happened. He left.'

'He continued his travels, perhaps?'

'There is no "he" to continue. When action is required, there is a "he". To love, to fight, to do, there is a "he". Otherwise, in terms of existence, there is no "he" or "him".'

'What does that mean? Does he still exist?'

'Yes, he does.'

Promontory and gorge unspool, snow-starched, cauterized.

'How does he exist? As a mountain of knowledge like Kailash? As a being?'

'In more ways than that.'

My mind is curiously blank. The air feels clarified, pre-verbal, intoxicating. It feels like the dawn of time, the beginning of the world, and I am asking questions of one of the ageless wise men, the lama of the tribe. This is all that seems to matter. The land is pared down to its bare bones – lake and mountain. We are pared down to archetype – disciple and master. This scene has been enacted in the past. It will be re-enacted in the future. Shiva's place of origin is not a pressing issue. At present, I'm not quite sure of my own.

'Could you explain?'

'You cannot typeset him into what you know as life. See, a human being becomes significant to you only in terms of what he or she can do or represent, isn't it? In that sense, he very much exists. One hundred per cent. What he knew, what he realized, the possibilities he held – he is able to make those happen through any number of people whenever he chooses, at any time in history, anywhere in the world. That means he exists.

'Is he going to walk as a nine-foot-tall man again? No, because that's not necessary. If it is necessary, he is capable of that also.'

'You speak with authority.'

'Everything that you know has come from a whole lot of people, right? I come from just one person. I only know what he said. I don't know anything else.'

'How many details of his actual life story can you retrieve?'

Sadhguru shrugs. 'All of it. But I'm not interested in Adiyogi's private life.'

'All the details, the particulars about his life, you could retrieve all of that?'

'Everything that happened fifteen thousand years ago, at this point maybe I cannot. But if I spend enough time on it, I could. Every detail, every step, every breath.'

'Is this the first time Adiyogi is being talked about in this way?'

'Right through the history of humanity, certain articulations have happened, sometimes in metaphor and sometimes in extreme devotion. Each articulation has been unique to its time. What I am saying to you now is partially relevant for today, and significantly more relevant for tomorrow.

'But nobody has articulated it in this kind of language, this mix of the symbolic and scientific, before. And that's because this is not me. This is not a man who grew up in the twentieth century talking to you. This is a man who is fifteen thousand years ago.'

'It's never been said this way before?'

'Always been said. Never been heard. He is not saying it just to me. Because I haven't made myself significant within myself, I hear what he says, that's all. He is saying it everywhere. He is saying it all the time. And that's because his voice is not his. It is the voice of existence.'

The mountains arch and stretch and lurch as the land continues to unravel – a wild moonscape howling with wind.

'When a Being beyond Time and Space touches you, you also become beyond Time and Space – the privilege of knowing "The Only Solution Is Dissolution".'

– SADHGURU

ISHA FOUNDATION

Isha Foundation is a non-profit human-service organization supported by millions of volunteers in over 250 centres worldwide. Recognizing the possibility of each person to empower another, Isha Foundation has created a massive movement that is dedicated to addressing all aspects of human well-being without ascribing to any particular ideology, religion or race. From its powerful Yoga programmes to its inspiring projects for society and environment, Isha's activities are designed to create an inclusive culture that is the basis for global harmony and progress.

Isha Foundation is also involved in several path-breaking outreach initiatives: Action for Rural Rejuvenation (ARR) enhances the quality of rural life through health care and disease prevention, community revitalization, women empowerment, the creation of sustainable livelihoods and Yoga programmes.

Isha Vidhya empowers rural children with quality education. Project GreenHands (PGH) initiates mass tree planting and creates a culture of care for the environment to keep this planet liveable for future generations.

Isha's unique approach to cultivating human potential has gained worldwide recognition and reflects in Isha Foundation's special consultative status with the Economic and Social Council (ECOSOC) of the United Nations.

http://isha.sadhguru.org
http://facebook.com/Sadhguru
http://youtube.com/Sadhguru
Twitter: @SadhguruJV